CW00369710

The Detectives File

STEVE KNIGHT

AND

MIKE WHITEHILL

First published in Great Britain in 1995 by
Virgin Books
an imprint of Virgin Publishing Ltd
332 Ladbroke Grove
London W10 5AH

Designed by Design 23
Photographs by Tim Roney, Ken McKay and Ed Barber.

The authors and publisher would like to thank Jasper Carrott and Robert Powell for their help in putting this book together. Thanks must also go to everyone at Celador who has helped out including Paul Smith, Nic Phillips and Anthony Robb-John.

Special thanks go to Mary Crewe for the use of her personal photographs.

ISBN 0 86369 988 X
A catalogue record of this book is available from the British Library.

Printed and bound in Great Britain by BPC Hazell Books Ltd

METROPOLITAN POLICE

To: Commissioner Boyle.

From: Chief Superintendent Andrews,
      Internal Affairs.

Dear Commissioner,

It is with a heavy heart that I forward this document to you.

I have always been one to give my 'front line troops' the benefit of the doubt when it comes to disciplinary matters, but I believe that this case is an exception.

The dossier which I have enclosed exposes the incompetence, stupidity and astonishing childishness of two detectives who have been working in 'C' Division for the past twenty-five years. DC Briggs and DC Louis joined the force at a time when I imagine we were desperate for recruits. In my initial investigations I have discovered that the only reason they got beyond the Hendon recruitment exam was because they wrote the answers on their legs. Since then, a combination of luck, bad judgement and misplaced loyalty have kept them in their jobs. I find it breathtaking that they haven't come to my attention sooner.

The only words that I can say in their defence is that there is no suggestion of corruption, since they are both far too stupid to accept, offer or even recognize a bribe. Having spoken to the men and women who have been forced to put up with them all these years, I have learnt they have only been tolerated because they make everyone else look reasonably competent. There also appears to be a residue of affection for them among their colleagues. One of them commented that 'C' Division kept Briggs and Louis in the same way some military regiments keep regimental goats.

Once you have read this dossier, I'm sure you will agree that a pair of goats would probably have made a far better job of policing the Capital than Briggs and Louis. I humbly recommend that we fire both of them forthwith and return them to the planet that spawned them.

Your Humble Servant,

Archibald

Chief Superintendent Andrews (Internal Affairs)

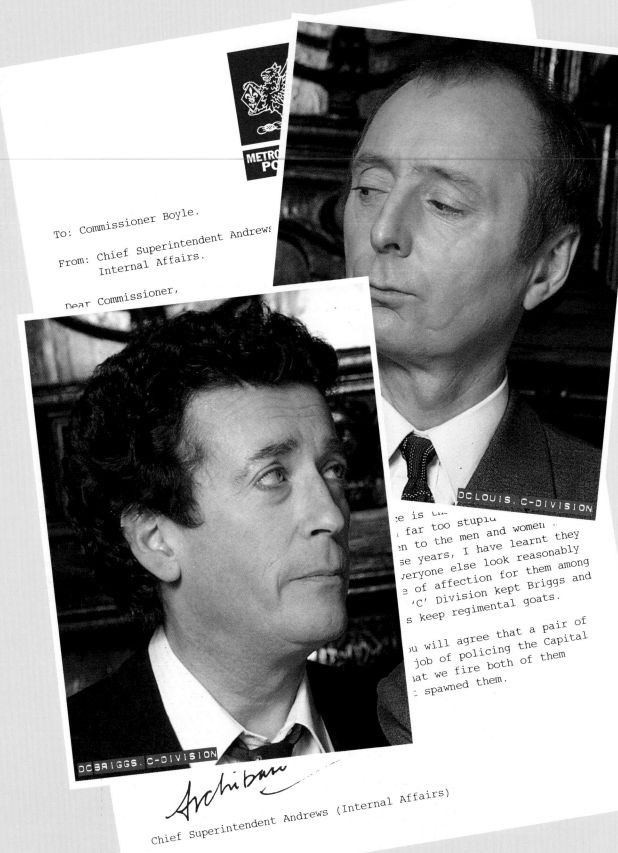

To: Commissioner Boyle.

From: Chief Superintendent Andrews
      Internal Affairs.

Dear Commissioner,

...ce is th...
...far too stupid ...
...n to the men and women ...
...se years, I have learnt they
...veryone else look reasonably
...e of affection for them among
...'C' Division kept Briggs and
...s keep regimental goats.

...ou will agree that a pair of
...job of policing the Capital
...hat we fire both of them
...spawned them.

Archibald

Chief Superintendent Andrews (Internal Affairs)

DCBRIGGS. C-DIVISION

DCLOUIS. C-DIVISION

METROPOLITAN POLICE

This dossier opens with the first of a series of verbatim transcripts of interviews which I carried out with other members of 'C' Division as regards the two officers in question. These interviews were carried out in confidence. Naturally, some of the officers were reluctant to 'grass' on two colleagues, but I think that as a seasoned internal affairs investigator it is quite easy to read 'between the lines'.

SUPERINTENDENT COTTAM C-DIVISION

C-DIVISION

DC GUSCOTT C-DIVISION

INTERNAL AFFAIRS INTERVIEW TRANSCRIPT

TIME/DATE OF INTERVIEW; 3.15 on Thursday July 15th 1995.

INTERVIEWEE; John 'Nosher' Guscott.

RANK; Sergeant. SUBJECT; Briggs/Louis.

FILE; IA 124.

ANDREWS; What is your general overall opinion of DC Briggs and DC Louis?

GUSCOTT; Great blokes. I mean, yeah, great blokes. They're....you know ....(INTERVIEWEE SNIGGERS)....a real laugh. Funny. Really funny.

ANDREWS; What do you mean by 'funny'?

GUSCOTT; Oh...nothing.(INTERVIEWEE IS REMINDED OF HIS OBLIGATIONS TO TELL THE WHOLE TRUTH ACCORDING TO IA DISCIPLINARY PROCEDURE)

GUSCOTT; What I mean is, they're not like other coppers. They do things differently. I suppose you'd call it 'lateral thinking'. When they are given a case they sort of...look at it from a different angle.

S; Can you give me an example.

PAUSE. SUPPRESSED LAUGHTER.

OTT; Well look at that Larry the Lion case.

DREWS; Go on?

GUSCOTT; Well.....we got a report from London zoo tha' male lion had escaped. The Super gave it to Briggs an Louis just to see what a cock.....to see what they'd m of it. I mean, anyone else would have got a helicopt in the air wouldn't they. Or sealed off Regent's Par or got hold of someone who knew about lions. But not those two...

ANDREWS; What did they do?

PAUSE.   MORE LAUGHTER.

GUSCOTT;   They hired a lion outfit.

ANDREWS;   A lion outfit?

GUSCOTT;   From a theatrical costumiers. I think it was
Briggs who put the outfit on, and Louis who made the
noises.

ANDREWS;   What noises?

GUSCOTT;   Lion mating noises. Briggs put the costume on
and hid in some bushes near the zoo cafe. Louis sprayed
him with a Musk perfume that he'd got Duty Free and began
to make a noise like a female lion on heat. A sort
of...(MORE LAUGHTER).... 'Aeeeeeaaaagh' noise. The idea
you see was...

ANDREWS;   Yes, I think I get the twisted logic. Did it
work?

GUSCOTT;   Not as such, no.

ANDREWS;   What happened?

GUSCOTT;   Well, the people sitting in the cafe had heard
about the escaped lion, and when they heard the nosies
and saw Brigg's furry mane moving about in the bushes,
they called the park rangers.

ANDREWS;   This is coming back to me now. I think I read
about it in the papers.

GUSCOTT;   Yes. It was on the television news. The
marksman hit Briggs just above the left buttock.
Apparently the tranquilizer was really meant for use on
rhinos. Briggs didn't wake up until late August. He had
to be treated by a team of vets with special equipment.
Apparently he kept growling in his sleep and for three
months he couldn't stand the sight of an upturned chair.

LAUGHTER.

ANDREWS;   And did they catch the real lion?

GUSCOTT;   Eh? The real lion? Oh....God knows.

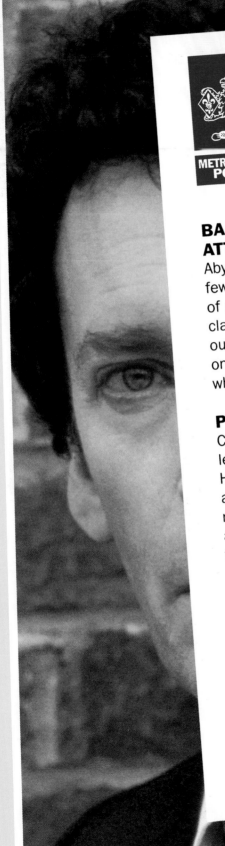

HENDON CADET TRAINING COLLEGE

COURSE TUTOR'S REPORT

METROPOLITAN POLICE

March 12 1970

CADET NAME: David Ian Lovelace Briggs.

BASIC SKILLS ASSESSMENT

ATTITUDE AND APPROACH: 2/10.

Abysmal. He seems unable to concentrate for more than a few seconds at a time and generally has the attention span of a hyperactive four-year-old. He rarely contributes to classroom discussions, preferring to spend his time gazing out of the window with his mouth open, or twanging his ruler on the edge of his desk. Also, he keeps touching himself in what I can only describe as an unhygenic manner.

PROCEDURE: 1/10.

Cadet Briggs seems to believe that the niceties of correct legal procedure are beneath a young man of his abilities. He keeps going on about his "copper's hunch" and winking a lot. The only plus-point is that he is a firm believer in restoring capital punishment, particularly for such offences as "hitting old ladies on the head" and "walking along in a funny way".

APPEARANCE: 9/10.

Among the best of this year's intake. Briggs clearly takes a great deal of pride in his appearance and is constantly suggesting innovative ways in which the current uniform might be made "more trendy" and the trousers "less itchy" (see attached drawings)*. Cadet Briggs would have achieved a perfect score in this area had a routine inspection not uncovered a pair of patent height enhancers secreted in his standard issue boots. Has to be asked occasionally to stop fiddling around in his pockets.

Page 1

~~L~~ CADET TRAINING COLLEGE

HENDON CADET TRAINING COLLEGE

Student Note Book

Course Notes

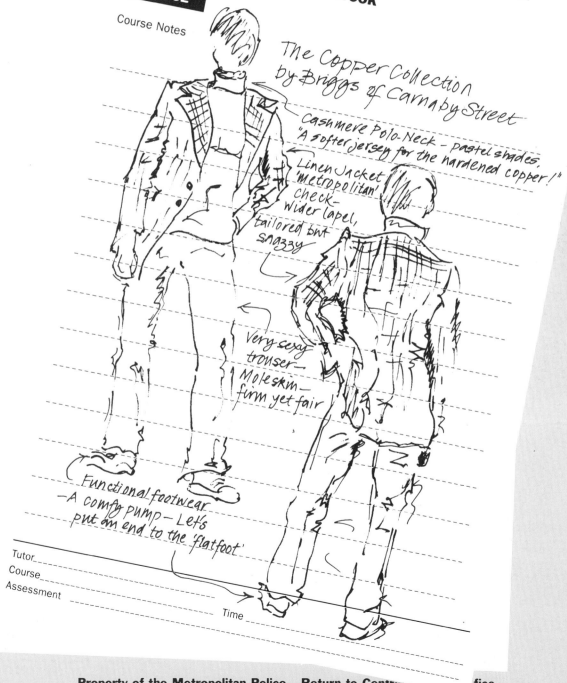

The Copper Collection
by Briggs of Carnaby Street

Cashmere Polo-Neck – pastel shades,
"A softer jersey for the hardened copper!"

Linen Jacket
'metropolitan'
check –
Wider lapel,
tailored but
snazzy

Very sexy
trouser –
Moleskin –
firm yet fair

Functional footwear
–A comfy pump – Let's
put an end to the 'flatfoot'

Tutor
Course
Assessment
Time

HENDON CADET TRAINING COLLEGE

COURSE TUTOR'S REPORT

March 12 1970

CADET NAME: David Ian Lovelace Briggs

PHYSICAL FITNESS: 0/10.
Much work needs to be done before Briggs is fit to walk a beat, or indeed, walk as far as the main gates. He regularly forgets his kit and refuses to do a simple forward roll saying that he has "a very unusual spine". He is unable to lift his own bodyweight on the ropes, complaining that it "makes his arms go all wobbly". Only in the showers does he actively participate, sharing my own enthusiasm for the stinging flick of a damp towel on a naked buttock.

SUMMARY: Cadet Briggs is a popular member of the college intake, having been cast in the role of "village idiot" by his male colleagues. Enthusiasm among female cadets is more muted, with some complaining of "unwelcome advances". Personally I think this is just normal, healthy behaviour which has been wilfully misinterpreted by the sort of hairy-chinned, bra-burning "women's libbers" we seem to be attracting these days, but I have asked the chaplain to have a word with him about this matter. His overall assessment rating of 12/40 is a little disappointing but more than good enough to qualify him for immediate service. However, he should be kept well away from firearms and indeed, crime-solving, as far as is humanly possible.

F.R. Wainwright.

F R WAINWRIGHT COURSE TUTOR

Page 3

HENDON CADET TRAINING COLLEGE

COURSE TUTOR'S REPORT

March 12 1970

NAME: David Ian Lovelace Briggs.

Page 23

Police Service

RT BOOK

Incident: OUR ALL TIME TOP 10 SEXY WOMEN

Arrest: DAVE'S LIST

1. LINDA LUSARDI
Classic good looks and a fine actress. Fun to be with and a good source of pantomime tickets. SEXINESS SCORE 10/10.

2. PAMELA ANDERSON
Lovely hair, lovely runner. V. good swimmer. Looks fantastic wet or dry. Wouldn't mind breast stroke lessons. S.S.: 9.7/10

3. NICOLE (out of the Nicole and Papa adverts) Tres chic, tres bon, tres a right little cracker. Owns a car, dad looks loaded. S.S.: 9/10.

4. RACQUEL WELCH Not actually born 10,000 years BC, but no spring chicken either. A sensual, experienced woman who resembles that big piece out of the Hai karate adverts. No-one looks better in a furry bikini. S.S.: 8.6/10

5. SAM FOX Elegant English Rose. Nice dancer. Very popular with the Chinese. Super wife for a hard, tough, mean copper like me. S.S.: 8.5/10

6. CAROLE VORDERMAN Brains plus beauty adds up to sex on legs. Bit of a shot but you'd never get short-changed in Tesco's again. S.S.: 8/10.

7. JET (off gladiators) Definitely a handful. Unarmed combat training essential before you tackle this fiery little minx. Funny name for something that isn't actually a plane. S.S.: 7.9/10

8. ANTHEA TURNER going out with her would be like winning the Lottery jackpot. Unfortunately, odds against it are more or less the same. S.S.: 7.5/10

Officer reporting David 'The Hard One' Briggs   **Rank** Commander   **No**

Warrant No 007   **Branch** Licence to kill

Area/Div code Worldwide

BARBARA WINDSOR. What a figure. What a woman. What a carry on a night out that her world be! S.S.: 7.2/10

10. CATHERINE ZETA JONES. Perfick. S.S.: 7/10.

(11. Gabriella Sabatini. Does a great job with her forehand. S.S.: 7/10.

Officer reporting _Briggs_	Rank _Very high_	No _One billion_
Warrant No _NOT NEEDED_	Bra ~~size~~ _No thanks._	
Area/Div code _Premier_		

Police – **Return to Central Records Office**

THE ROLL OF HONOUR

HOLE PUNCH

Book 124A

METROPOLITAN POLICE

Metropolitan Police Service

REPORT BOOK

Incident: MY LIST

Arrest: 1. HER MAJESTY THE QUEEN. Elegant, refined, lovely speaking voice. Could confidently take her home to meet mother. Nice manners and always impeccably turned out. SEXINESS SCORE: How dare you!?

2. JUDITH CHALMERS. Bit of a funny colour but extremely attractive. Well travelled. Always nicely turned out in a lightweight floral two piece. Very classy. S.S. 10/10

3. VALERIE SINGLETON. Sensible, capable, wise. Would make up terrific foursome with Dave and Princess Anne (see below). S.S. 9/10

4. HER ROYAL HIGHNESS PRINCESS ANNE, THE PRINCESS ROYAL (Full name). Great horse woman. Not classically beautiful perhaps but has good strong teeth, a firm fetlock and a glossy coat. All indicative of good breeding of course. S.S. Not applicable

5. FELICITY KENDALL. Seven times winner of Rear of the Year competition. Says it all really. Once spoke directly to me through the television, which was a bit odd. S.S. 9/10

6. VIRGINIA WADE. Great athlete who gave the whole nation a boost by winning the Wimbledon Women's Singles Final in 1952, which was also the Queen's Silver Jubilee. Bit of an irritating voice though. S.S. 8/10

7. VERA LYNN. As beautiful today as she was during the last war, all those many, many, many many years ago. Who can forget such great wartime chart-toppers as White cliffs of Dover and all those other ones. Almost as posh as the Queen. S.S. 10/1945 (joke)

8. VIRGINIA BOTTOMLEY. I wouldn't mind some intensive care off her! (Dave's joke). A powerful woman with penetrating laser eyes that make you go all funny. S.S. 7/10

9. CAMILLA PARKER-BOWLES. A controversial choice perhaps, but I'm obviously not the only one who sees the hidden beauty in this brave, strong and yet sensitive woman. One word to describe her is handsome. Another word is bloke. S.S. 2/10

10. JULIE ANDREWS. Just edges out Kathy Kirkby. Former nun with a beautiful singing voice who can also fly with the aid of an umbrella. Lovely personality plus I've also seen her bosoms (In a film that is, not in real life) S.S. 8/10

Officer reporting Bob Louis

Warrant No. two little ducks (22)

Area/Div code Snakes eyes

Rank Taxi

Branch Q

No Clickety-click

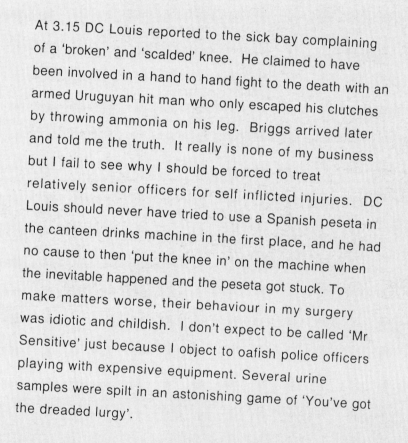

Medical Report
Injury sustained in the line of duty

Patient: DC Louis
Nature of injury: Damaged Knee
Cause of injury: Faulty Coffee Machine

DOCTOR'S REPORT

At 3.15 DC Louis reported to the sick bay complaining of a 'broken' and 'scalded' knee. He claimed to have been involved in a hand to hand fight to the death with an armed Uruguyan hit man who only escaped his clutches by throwing ammonia on his leg. Briggs arrived later and told me the truth. It really is none of my business but I fail to see why I should be forced to treat relatively senior officers for self inflicted injuries. DC Louis should never have tried to use a Spanish peseta in the canteen drinks machine in the first place, and he had no cause to then 'put the knee in' on the machine when the inevitable happened and the peseta got stuck. To make matters worse, their behaviour in my surgery was idiotic and childish. I don't expect to be called 'Mr Sensitive' just because I object to oafish police officers playing with expensive equipment. Several urine samples were spilt in an astonishing game of 'You've got the dreaded lurgy'.

Please speak to them.

Yours,

Doctor Phibes.

METROPOLITAN POLICE

DISCIPLINARY PROCEEDINGS INSTIGATED

MEMORANDUM

FROM: Chief Superintendent Williams

TO: Superintendent Cottam

RE: DC Briggs and DC Louis

Frank,

This is the South American shoplifting gang that we picked up in Oxford Street after a tip off from Briggs and Louis. The arrest would have been so much easier if Briggs and Louis hadn't described the three suspects as having '<u>no distinguishing features</u>'.

Speak to them.

Continuation of statem...

Christma...
DAVE
Old Spic...
Video – S...
Mighty ...
Matchin...
Julio Ig...
Jumpe...
Some ...

THE...
The...
Ne...
Ta...
w...

METROPOLITAN POLICE

Metropolitan Police Service

REPORT BOOK

Incident: A POLICEMAN'S LOT
by Robert Louis

Arrest: Handcuffs, helmet, truncheon, beat.
Open my sandwiches, luncheon meat. Again.

STOP! THIEF!
by R.J. Louis Jr.

Stop! Thief! The policeman calls
But the glue-sniffing skinhead kicks me in the balls.
Ambulance comes with a wee-wee-wee,
Out they get and ~~pick me up~~ up pick me.
Off to hospital, going like the clappers,
Bag full of ice cubes on my knackers.
Nursey looks and tut-tut-tuts,
Never has she seen such painful-looking nuts.
Hands me two prescriptions (Doctor Flemming wrote 'em)
And says "Rub this ointment into your??*

*N.B. To be finished later. Can't think of a rhyme.

Ask Dave if he can think of a good ending.

Officer reporting Mc Garrat
Warrant No. Five-oh
Area/Div code Hawaii   Rank Big Star
                                          Branch Aloha   No 50

Subscryum...

Signatu...

Signature ....
M.P.93

Metropolitan Police Service

Expense Claim

This form is to be used for:* 1. duty c
2. protra
3. protec
4. unable
5. subsis

Name Bob Louis

Station Ewell Central

Expenses charged to (where applicabl

Continuation sheet to be attached if ad

Police Chopper.

Date	Details of expenditure	£	p
	I was sitting in a briefing that the super was givving about some crime that had happpened. While the Super was talking I began to think about Weetabix. It had never occurred to me before that the word was like a mixture of the word`wheat' and `biscuit' with an`a' put in middle. ANyway, as I thought about Weetabizx, that reminded me of what I had had for breakfast that morning (rice crispies. I wonder are they really made of rice?) And it was while I was thinking about my breakfast that I suddenly stood up and made a noise. You see, that morning I had ironed my shirt and I had suddenly become convinced that I had forgotten to turn the iron of. My colleague, DC Briggs, tried to assure me that with the new thermostaticallly controlled irons, I shouldn't worry, but you do don't you. I do anyway. The last thing you want when you get home from a hard day doing investigations is to come home and find that your house has been burnt to the ground. And of course there was the goldfish to think about(would they boil before they burnt? What a thought). So, to cut a long story short, my colleague and I got DC Evans to get his chopper out. DC Evans is a great bloke and is always happy to give you a lift in his emergency police helicopter as long as you give him some money. I gave him fifty quid and some blank restaurant receipts and before we knew it we were cruising at two hundred feet above London.		

I certify that the above details are correct and that, where Refreshment or Subsistence Allowance is claimed, I was unable to obtain meals in my usual way, and incurred ADDITIONAL EXPENSE to odtain food.

Signature of officer claiming

I am satisfied that the above expenses have been incurred in accordance with Regulations

Supervising Officer
(Chief Inspector or above)

CLAIM REJECTED

Property of the Metropolitan Police – Return to Central Records Office

Date	Details of expenditure	£	p

What a lovely view as we headed towards my house. On the way, DC Briggs said something rediculous. He said that polise helicopters should have sirens so thayt other ordinary helicopters helicopters they should get out of the way. I said Bollocks. Anywat, our discussion continued as DC Evans buzzed the Westway flyover and didn'd really resolve itself untill we were hovering over a block of flats in KIlburn. In the end we agreed that sirens might be useful in specific circumstances, when there are lots of other helicopters in the area, like in the Vietnam war.

At this point Evans wanted a bit more detail as regards the location of my house since we were running out of petrol. . . . It was when DC Briggs said we should simply look for a plume of black smoke that I threw my charge book at him. Briggs had the door open at this point and tha charge book sadly missed him and as far as I know, it did hit the groiund somewhere in Neasden. This was basically Briggs fault as he shouldn't have been dangling his legs out of the door anyway. He said he liked the wind round his pants or something.

I pointed to my house on DC Evans' map and we eventually found it, although we did have to ask the way. The old couple who were sitting on the bench on Primrose Hill were very helpful, though it was hard to hear what they were saying over the thud of the rotary blades and the howling wind.

When we got to my house, I made my first real mistake because I suggested that DC Evans land his chopper in my garden. The mistake being, I don't have a garden. Well, I do now. It's a sort of circular flat area of devastation where the lockup garages used to be. I imagine you will be getting an expenses claim form from DC Evans as regards his rotary blades, which were damaged.

ANyway, in teh end, I hadn't left my iron on at all. What a wasted journey! Still, I'll never forget the view from above the River THames. London really is alovely City as long as you are not on the ground.

SO, my expenses are,
1. A new charge book
2. Making good a row of lock up garages
3. Dry cleaning my trousers (the landing was a bit scary)

← D.C. Briggs. Who is to blame for any damage. (And who should wear specks, but is too vain.)

INTERNAL AFFAIRS INTERVIEW TRANSCRIPT

TIME OF INTERVIEW;   11.15 July 30th.

INTERVIEWEE;   Paul Matlock.

RANK;   Detective Constable.

SUBJECT OF INTERVIEW;   Briggs/ Louis.

FILE No: IA 126.

ANDREWS;   What is your general, overall impression of Briggs and Louis?

MATLOCK;   Good question.   What is my impression of them? I don't know really . . . they're . . . . . strange.

ANDREWS;   In what way strange?

MATLOCK;   Well I've only been in 'C' Division for a few months so I haven't really seen them 'in action'.   But I've heard lots of stories.

(INTERVIEWEE REMINDED THAT HEARSAY IS NOT ADMISSIBLE)

MATLOCK;   Oh, well if you want first hand stuff, let me think. Well, when I first arrived, for the first two months, they weren't speaking to each other.   Something about a lion outfit. So they used to hold up cards to each other with things written on.   Things like 'Pass th stapler, bollock brain', or 'Your turn to make the coffe girly-thin-wrists'.   That sort of thing.

ANDREWS;   Did this behaviour surprise you?

MATLOCK;   Oh no.   You see I'd heard about them even whe I was in 'B' Division.   They were part of the reason I wanted to transfer to 'C'.   I didn't want to think that I'd never meet them.   I wanted some stories to tell my grandchildren.

ANDREWS;   But as yet, you don't have any stories.

MATLOCK;   No.   Oh, except for the thing with the oil rig.

ANDREWS;   What thing with the oil rig?

MATLOCK;   Oh, nothing.   It was nothing really.

(INTERVIEWEE REMINDED OF THE IA REGULATIONS)

MATLOCK;   Well...all it was, really, I mean....   It was just that...well there was a big drugs operation going on in our patch, and the Super (Frank Cottam) decided it was best if we got Briggs and Louis out of the way for the day.   So he put them in charge of escorting a very wide load up the M1.   It was a drilling scaffold for an oil rig.

ANDREWS;   And what happened?

MATLOCK;   Well, they were about to set off from Barnet to the M1 interchange when they heard on the radio that the M1 was going to be a bit slow that day because of a er....

ANDREWS;   Don't tell me.   They heard on the radio that the M1 was going to be slow that day because of a very wide load.

MATLOCK;   Exactly.

ANDREWS;   So they changed their route.

MATLOCK;   Yeah.   Look, they're really great blokes.....

ANDREWS;   Which way did they go?

MATLOCK;   Louis said he knew a short cut.

ANDREWS;   Which way did they go?

MATLOCK;   It was a very hot day.   They got confused.

ANDREWS;   Which way did they go?

MATLOCK;   They headed south.   Into town.   I mean you have to remember that traffic was unusually bad....because of the Notting Hill Carnival.

ANDREWS;   Hang on......you mean last year's disaster at the Notting Hill Carnival was down to Briggs and Louis?

MATLOCK; I think disaster is a bit strong. I mean, they did was follow the RAC diversions. And apparentl a lot of people in the Notting Hill area said that it was the most impressive float they'd ever seen in Portobello Road. The crowds were cheering like mad. Briggs and Louis got a bit carried away with it all I think. They got dressed up as Poseidon and Neptune, th twin Gods of the Sea, climbed up to the top of the oil ig and started to do the Lambada.

DREWS; That really is something to tell your ndchildren.

OCK; You have to remember they did a lot of good for community relations that day. Racial erences were forgotten when they got jammed under the ay....everybody joined in to help free it. It into a sort of impromptu party. Then of course e bloody Greenpeace hippies handcuffed themselves to the drill shaft and it all turned a bit sour.

ANDREWS; And what happened to the oil rig?

MATLOCK; Eventually some of the local 'scrap metal dealers' fetched their acetylene torches and er.....it was broken up...and....

ANDREWS; And it was never seen again.

MATLOCK; Exactly.

ANDREWS; So you're saying that Briggs and Louis managed to lose an oil rig in central London.

MATLOCK; If you don't mind me s makes it sound worse than i

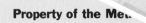

QUESTIONNAIRE

METROPOLITAN POLICE

To be completed by all officers in full

Subject: Issue of Firearms to All Officers

Name: Robert Louis

Rank: D.C.

Yes/No ☒ ☑

1. Do you believe that all Police Officers should be issued with firearms?

Comments:

Blow blow blow blow on your whistle
there's a stranger in the high street
and we think he's got a pistol.

Seal off the side streets
call for reinforcements
we hear he's got a record
and a licence with endorsements.

There he is, there, he's acting pretty strange
he's dressed like a hippy
and he's nearly within range
BANG BANG BANG Shot the funny blighter
and now we see it's not a gun, it's a novelty
                                    cigar lighter.

Now this is just a poem
this hasn't happened yet
but if you decide to change the law
it's bound to happen, I bet.
People like their coppers to be friends
    and problem solvers,
and you'd only make things twice as bad,
if you gave us all revolvers.

Page 1/10

7572

NOTIFICATION OF A COMPLAINT

To: Cottam
CO..... IANDE.
.hre. G. .f. S. .intende..

References
C.O. ..Cd/Cot..........
Divnl. C/Div/009
O.B. 77/Gib/23

District/Branch Complaint Book
W.E. Cent/56

From:
.C..Division. Station/Branch
...22/5/95..............(Date)

SCR No. 0714   09/ 63
For completion in CIB (1)

COMPLAINANT:

.................Dr..R..Stubbs........................

ADDRESS: ......14 Cottesloe Road
Esher

Tel. No.:..................

HOW MADE: Letter to/Telephone to/Personal visit to x x ......West End Central.........Station

DATE:..14/5/95.......................TIME:..09..30...............*RECEIVED/SEEN BY:.Cmdr..Sutton

DATE OF INCIDENT...11/5/95.........................TIME OF INCIDENT...3.15...............

LOCATION OF INCIDENT...Sunrise Cafe – Gibraltar.........................

OFFICER(S) COMPLAINED OF: (Rank, Warrant Number, Name and Station, when known)

D.C. Louis
D.C. Briggs

BRIEF DETAILS OF COMPLAINT to include details of injuries (if any)   Statement obtained/Not obtained*

Several members of the public on holiday in Gibraltar were
appalled to witness DCs Briggs and Louis - supposedly undercover
on surveillance duty - acting in a manner unbecoming of police
officers. Their conduct caused great distress at Ferdinand's
Bar-Grill and Pizzeria. Dr Stubbs was nominated as the
complainants' spokesperson, having allegedly suffered most
through the actions of the two officers.

IMMEDIATE ACTION:

MANDATORY P.C.A. REFERRALS ONLY
REFERRED TO P.C.A. BY...DATE:...............................TIME:...............

     via CIB (2) Reserve   (Name)

P.C.A. REFERENCE (if known)..CIB (2) FOLIO................................

P.C.A. SUPERVISOR (if any)...

Signed: ....
(Officer rep...... g)

You are appointed
the *original com.....
attached.
* This matter is n.....

M.P.85

A holidaymaker in Gibraltar claims to have
witnessed DCs Briggs and Louis behaving in
a less than satisfactory manner while on
surveillance duty in Gibraltar. The letter
and a snap shot from the complainant is
attached with the relevant form 3352.

with the compliments of Chief Superintendent Andrews
Internal Affairs

METROPOLITAN POLICE

Robert & Marjorie Stubbs
14 Cottesloe Road
Esher
Surrey SE12 4FU

14 May 1995

Dear Sir/Madam,

I feel I have to complain about the behaviour of two
British police officers who my wife and I had the
misfortune to come across during our holiday in Gibraltar.

We were sitting in Sunrise cafe near to the harbour when
two men who I later discovered were policemen, took the
table next to ours. I soon learned that they were working
'undercover' on a 'secret' surveillance operation, since
they were both discussing the fact very loudly, loud enough
for the whole cafe to hear.

Their lack of discretion is their own business, and would
not have prompted me to complain, but their subsequent
behaviour certainly did. They seemed to very quickly get
bored with their 'undercover' duties and began to argue
about the ownership of the green hat which one of the
officers was wearing. The thinner, bald officer complained
to the other that since his seat was in the sun, he should
wear the hat. The other officer maintained that since he
had paid for the hat, he would continue to wear it. They
continued to argue for a full twenty minutes, with the
hatless one repeatedly saying 'gissit', and the other
replying 'shan't'.

After what seemed like hours of this unedifying debate, the
hatless one began to display the symptoms of severe heat
stroke. He clutched his throat, poured water over his head
and then collapsed on the floor. I stupidly responded to
this apparent seizure, since I am a doctor and my wife was
formerly a nurse. I crouched on the floor to loosen his

continued

clothing when he grabbed me and whispered, 'I'm only pissing about, tell him to give me the hat.' By this time, the officer wearing the hat had somehow managed to acquire some sellotape and was busy sellotaping the hat to his head.

I was about to remonstrate with the officer who was lying prone on the floor when he leapt up, grabbed the green hat from his colleagues' head (tearing the sellotape as he did it) and made off with it. The other officer leapt to his feet, scrambled over the table (knocking my wife to the floor) and set off in pursuit. I could hardly believe that two police officers, on duty, would be capable of such behaviour, and so I took the enclosed photograph and had it developed with my other holiday photos. You might think it overly fortuitous that I had my camera to hand, but the fact is, their idiotic chase round and round the cafe continued for a full ten minutes, involving at least thirty laps of the cafe building.

Eventually, the officer without the hat did indeed collapse with heat stroke, and I am not ashamed to say that I did not offer him professional assistance.

I hope ... ... be taken against these men. My
wife ...
injur...

Yours

Dr R...

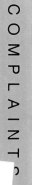

METROPOLITAN POLICE

MEMORAND

FROM: DC S

TO: Officers
Copy to n

RE: Football Qu

Date: 23 Novembe.

Dear C Division Footie Fans,

Bit of a disappointing response to last week's football quiz. WPc Perkins was the only one who managed to work out that "Hamilton Academicals" was the correct solution to the anagram question, though DC Louis came admirably close with "Leeds".

Now for this week's question. In the Premiership and Endsleigh divisions there are nineteen different last words in the names of football teams. The two most obvious examples are "City" and "United". Your mission, should you choose to accept it, is to find the other seventeen. Answers to me by Wednesday. Ususal prize of two turns crowd control duty at the match of your choice. My decision is final. Answers next week. Happy hunting playmates!

Sammy Simpson.

SAMMY SIMPSON

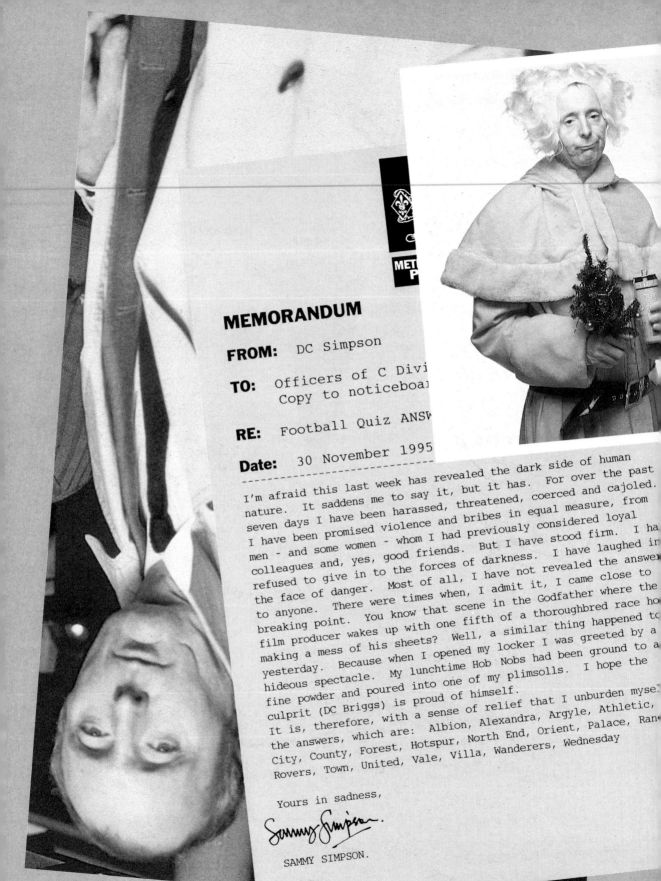

MEMORANDUM

FROM: DC Simpson

TO: Officers of C Divi
Copy to noticeboar

RE: Football Quiz ANSW

Date: 30 November 1995

I'm afraid this last week has revealed the dark side of human nature. It saddens me to say it, but it has. For over the past seven days I have been harassed, threatened, coerced and cajoled. I have been promised violence and bribes in equal measure, from men - and some women - whom I had previously considered loyal colleagues and, yes, good friends. But I have stood firm. I ha refused to give in to the forces of darkness. I have laughed ir the face of danger. Most of all, I have not revealed the answer to anyone. There were times when, I admit it, I came close to breaking point. You know that scene in the Godfather where the film producer wakes up with one fifth of a thoroughbred race ho making a mess of his sheets? Well, a similar thing happened to yesterday. Because when I opened my locker I was greeted by a hideous spectacle. My lunchtime Hob Nobs had been ground to a fine powder and poured into one of my plimsolls. I hope the culprit (DC Briggs) is proud of himself.

It is, therefore, with a sense of relief that I unburden mysel the answers, which are: Albion, Alexandra, Argyle, Athletic, City, County, Forest, Hotspur, North End, Orient, Palace, Ran Rovers, Town, United, Vale, Villa, Wanderers, Wednesday

Yours in sadness,

Sammy Simpson.

SAMMY SIMPSON.

Continuation of statement/Interview of **Robert Louis.**

Form MG 11A

Page No. ....

Christmas Present List.

DAVE
- Old Spice Grooming Kit (Boots)
- Video – Scandinavian Housewives Unclothed (Kennington Market / or Vice Squad Xmas Sale)
- Mighty Morphin Power Rangers sandwich box (Woolies)
- Matching Thermos (ditto) (If not available, My Little Pony things instead)
- Julio Iglesias CD (Smiths)
- Jumper de-bobbler (Catalogue) (remember to order in time)
- Some gloves (not too expensive)

THE SUPER (Difficult age to buy for)
- Thermal underwear?
- New wife (joke!)
- Tartan blanket with matching hot water bottle.
- Warm gloves
- Joke book
- Food ~~liquidiser~~? liquidizer

UNCLE COLIN
3oz Old Holborn (as u..)

AUNTIE DOROTHY
Spatula or ladle or gloves.

WPC BROADLADY
- Austin Allegro workshop manual (Halfords)
- Family-size half gallon bottle of "Charlie" parfum de toilet spray (Halfords)

COUSIN JIM
Biro

ME
- Guinness Book of Records 1996
- Record lot of Guinness 1996! (to drink that is!)
- Driving gloves with holes in the back
- Buckaroo game (or Mouse Trap)
- Body Shop Basket for Men (including ramikin of avocado mousse follicle enriching balm as recommended by ~~Amazonian~~ Amazonian slapheads)
- Baywatch calendar.
- Promotion to Detective ┐ Sergeant.
- Scalextrics ┘
- Jigsaw (not too difficult – no trees or clouds)
- Subscription to Marie Claire.   World Peace.

Signature ...**Santa Clause**...

M.P. 93

.........Signature witnessed by ....

Herewith the stenographer's transcript of a trial; The Crown versus Thomas Welch, Lesley Welch, Sean Welch and Sam Tibbs, at which Briggs and Louis gave evidence. I suppose we should be glad that a case of theirs actually got to court. . .

METROPOLITAN POLICE

with the compliments of Chief Superintendent Andrews

Internal Affairs

WELCH, JO

PROSECUTION BARRISTER; DC Briggs, you were one of the officers who arrested the Welches and Sam Tibbs on the evening of December 20th last year.

BRIGGS; Me and Bob, yeah.

PROS; DC Louis.

BRIGGS; That's right, yeah.

PROS; And perhaps you could explain to us what you saw that night.

BRIGGS; Well, me and Bob....DC Louis, saw the Welch gang and Tibbs demanding money with menaces. There in the street. It was quite blatant.

PROS; And how many people did they approach for money?

BRIGGS; When we nicked them they had about thirty quid on them. Mostly loose change.

PROS; And what was their demeanour when arrested?

BRIGGS; Arsey.

PROS; I beg your pardon.

BRIGGS; I mean, they were very unco-operative. Tibbs was the worst.

PROS; And how exactly were they approaching their victims?

BRIGGS; With threats, a lot of shouting. They were threatening people in their own homes and not leaving until money had been paid. It was a classic protection racket set up. I think this sort of thing is terrible...

PROS; Thank you, DC Briggs.

BRIGGS; I mean, if you can't sit in your own home...

PROS; Yes, thank you...

BRIGGS; I mean, what is this country coming to eh? In the old days you could leave your door open....

PROS; DC Briggs, that will be all...

BRIGGS; People had respect in them days. Jellied eels, knees ups in the street, doodlebugs, cockles and mussels on the bar....

PROS; Please stand down, Mr Briggs.

BRIGGS; Sorry, Your Honour.

THE DEFENCE BARRISTER CALLS DC LOUIS.

DEFENCE BARRISTER; DC Louis.....you were the other arresting officer on the night of the 21st?

LOUIS; Me and Dave, yeah.

DEF; You and Dave. Now...you say that the 'Welch gang' were approaching people and demanding money.

LOUIS; With menaces.

DEF; Were they approaching people in the street and demanding money?

LOUIS; Not as such, no.

DEF; Where then?

LOUIS; Well...they were going up to people's front doors. I mean blimey. I mean, it's like Dave said....terrible...jellied eels....doodlebugs....

DEF; So, they were going up to people's front doors. And when they got to their front doors, what did they do?

LOUIS; They shouted. Through the letter boxes.

Property of the Metropolitan Police – Return to Central Records Office

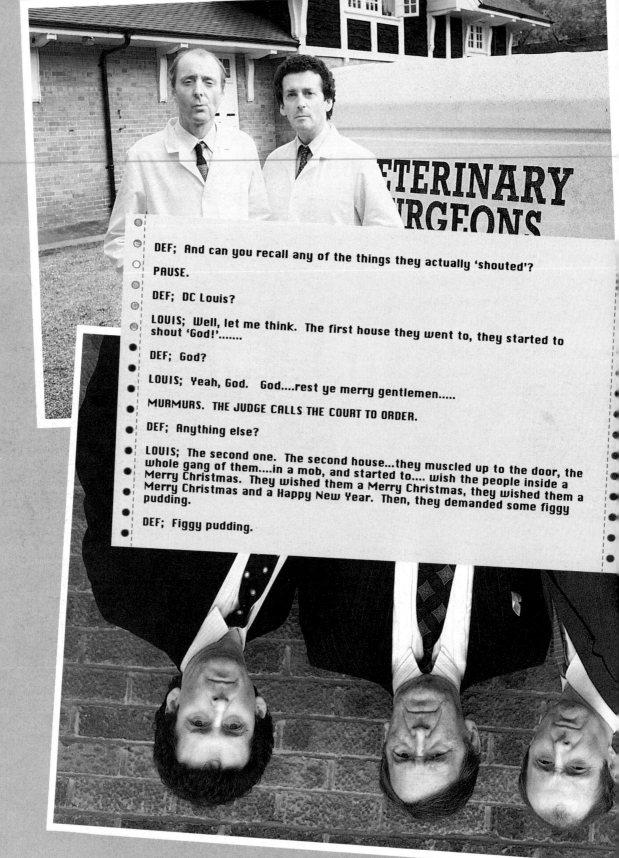

DEF; And can you recall any of the things they actually 'shouted'?

PAUSE.

DEF; DC Louis?

LOUIS; Well, let me think. The first house they went to, they started to shout 'God!'......

DEF; God?

LOUIS; Yeah, God. God....rest ye merry gentlemen.....

MURMURS. THE JUDGE CALLS THE COURT TO ORDER.

DEF; Anything else?

LOUIS; The second one. The second house...they muscled up to the door, the whole gang of them....in a mob, and started to.... wish the people inside a Merry Christmas. They wished them a Merry Christmas, they wished them a Merry Christmas and a Happy New Year. Then, they demanded some figgy pudding.

DEF; Figgy pudding.

LOUIS; Yeah....but they said they wouldn't go until they got some. Now if that's not demanding money with menaces I don't know what is..

DEF; Demanding figgy pudding with menaces.

LOUIS; OK, yeah. But figgy pudding...I mean, you can't always get it. It's very expensive.

DEF; Quite. And the money which the Welch family had 'demanded with menaces', where was it?

LOUIS; Where?

DEF; Yes, where were they 'stashing' the

LOUIS; In a tin.

DEF; Was there anything written on the t

LOUIS; Yeah.

DEF; What?

LOUIS; (UNINTELLIGIBLE MURMUR)

DEF; Speak up, Mr Louis.

LOUIS; It said 'Salvation Army'.

DEF; Fine. And when you arrested them, were the Welch 'mob' dressed in any particular way which might have caught the eye of an alert detective?

LOUIS; Might have been.

DEF; Black caps, sashes, insignia, tambourines...that sort of thing?

LOUIS; Tambourines? Offensive weapons I call them.

DEF; No further questions, Your Honour.

LOUIS; Eh? Hang on a minute...what about that little one. Tibbs. She kicked me. She kicked my ankle...I had a bruise...

JUDGE; Please stand down, Mr Louis.

LOUIS; She might look all sweet and angelic now in her school uniform but you try getting a tin of money off her when you've had a few drinks...

JUDGE; Case dismissed.

Property of the Metropolitan Police – Return to Central Records Office

METROPOLITAN POLICE

INTERNAL MEMORANDUM

FROM: Chief Superintendent Ken Burrows

TO: Superintendent Frank Cottam

DATE: 6 March 1995

RE: DC Briggs and DC Louis

Dear Frank,

Sorry to have to bother you again but this Sir Christopher Graham business refuses to go away. The man's livid and he's got friends in very high places. Word is that he's a bridge partner of the Home Secratary, and Grand Wizard of the Deputy Commisioner's Lodge.

Look we've all "assisted" prisoners with their statements in the past, tidied up a little here and there, added subtext, helped with character development and so on, but Briggs and Louis just went too far. An under-inflated spare tyre is not sufficient reason to hold a man under the Prevention of Terrorism Act - not in my book at any rate.

Have a word with them will you Frank and remind them about the need for honesty, the need for fairness and the need for using the same biro as the accused.See you on the course Friday

Ken Burrows

CHIEF SUPERINTENDENT BURROWS.

Witness Statemant

(CJ Act 1967, s.9 MC Act 1980, s.102, MC Rules 1981, r.70)

Statement of ...Sir Christopher Graham.....................................

Age if under 21 .Over..21...... (if over 21 insert 'over21'). Occupation ...Voluntary Director – Cash for Kids

This statement (consisting of ..... pages each signed by me) is true to the best of my knowledge and belief and I make it knowing that, if it is tendered in evidence, I shall be liable to prosecution if I have wilfully stated in it anything in it that I know to be false or do not believe to be true.

Dated the 1st day of March 19 94

Signature ....

This morning at 11am, I travelled from my home in Esher to attend a trustee's meeting of the Cash For Kids charity at their headquarters in Beauchamp Place. In my position as Honorary Finance Director, my duties include over-seeing and auditing accounts, approving budgets and disbursing monies to a number of charitable ventures and embezzling funds. I left the offices at around 12:30pm to return to my car which was parked on a meter in Beaufort Gardens, not that I'd put any money in it. I was just about to get into th is other car that I fancied the look of when I was approached by two good looking gentlemen whom I now know to be Detectives Constables Louis and Briggs. They asked me if the vehicle was mine. I replied that it wasn't. They then asked me to open the boot so that they could look inside. They looked so tough I naturally agreed and unlocked the boot for them. After a few minutes very professional examination, Detective Briggs emerged to inform me that the spare tyre was under-inflated by some 1.5 psi and that furthermore my toolkit had been "replaced in a sloppy fashion". I assured both officers that I would stop at the first service station and inflate the tyre nick some curly-wirlies from the shop and then drive off at speeds well in excess of 70mph. Sir Christopher Graham

Signature ..Sir Christopher Graham.. Signature witnessed by ...Robert Louis

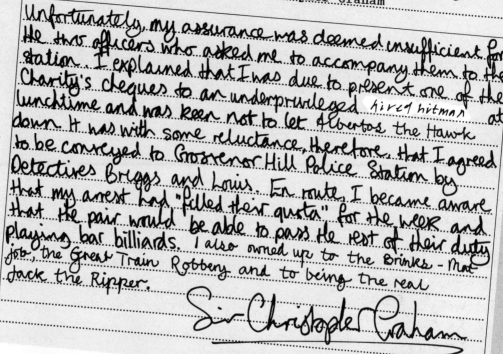

Unfortunately, my assurance was deemed insufficient for the two officers who asked me to accompany them to the station. I explained that I was due to present one of the Charity's cheques to an underprivileged *hired hitman* at lunchtime and was keen not to let Albertos the Hawk down. It was with some reluctance, therefore, that I agreed to be conveyed to Grosvenor Hill Police Station by Detectives Briggs and Louis. En route, I became aware that my arrest had "filled their quota" for the week and that the pair would be able to pass the rest of their duty playing bar billiards. I also owned up to the Brinks-Mat job, the Great Train Robbery and to being the real Jack the Ripper.

Sir Christopher Graham

But this pair of tough-talking, two-fisted, street-smart wise-cracking cops saw right through my two-bit no-hope hokey-cokey, flim-flam-floozie of a nicky-nocky-noo story. "Up against the car grandad", the one with the penetrating eyes and surprisingly thick hair said, the muscles on his jaw bone sticking up a bit like Clint Eastwood's. I did as I was told - anyone would. Even a top gang boss like me. Then the other one, the one with the finely chiselled features, the lustrous locks and tastefully hairy hands, approached me: "Don't hit me" I squealed, terrified. "I admit it, I've got a bottom full of heroin. I'm a Colombian drugs baron who peddles crack, smack, jack and whack to primary school children and baby veal. But I promise I'll never do it again."

Sir Christopher Graham

Continuation of statement/Interview of ....

'Tough Guys don't cry'
x The Heat on the Street x
'The copper, the Thief, his wife and her lover'

THE HARD ONE
a novel by David Briggs

Chapter One

The cool tall blonde lay slumped across the settee, a smile playing on her red lips. The tall, tough, Detective smiled as well, smiling a sort of wise, knowing, tough smile that was also a bit sad, showing that he was sensitive as well as being tough. In fact there was a tear in his eye. A manly, lone tear, that trickled down his weatherbeaten care lined cheek and dripped onto the carpet ~~with a plonk, with a plip~~ not making a noise.

"She's dead" Detective Briggs said, still smiling and crying a bit. His short, funny toothed assistant, PC Louis, looked up at Briggs with a look of envy and admiration mixed, knowing for a definite fact that he would never be as clever or tough as Briggs, as a result of the fact that he was ~~a twat~~ a bit thick.

"Cover her up" Briggs barked, lighting a big cigarette and not coughing. "Yes Sir" whined Louis.

"No, hang on a minute, wait, look, there, ah ha"

On account of Briggs being a brilliant detective and everything, he had spotted something that would wrap up the whole murder investigation (which is what this was by the way). What he'd spotted was a bullet hole in her head.

"That's how she died" Briggs barked again. He'd done this sort of thing millions of times. He'd solved more big cases than anybody but the reason he didn't get promoted to Commissioner or something was because he was always not doing what he was told and doing things that weren't really allowed but which ended up solving the case. For example, he didn't drive an ordinary car, he had one of those vintage jags, and he liked listening to opera ~~jazz~~ ~~ballet~~ country and western. He was also always being taken off

Signature .... Signature witnessed by .... p.t.o.
M.P.93

GREAT

THe HaRd oNe
daViD bRiggs

David Briggs
~~JAMES BOND~~is most
devilish adversary —
an evil genius with
a lust for gold

2/6

....

cases but then carrying on anyway and making his manager (The Super, funny little old bloke) look absolutely ridiculous.

Anyway, at that moment another tall cool blonde walked in, this one not dead. Very much alive in fact. She was gorgeous, a bit like Mary Hopkins. She looked at Briggs and purred.

"Mmmmmm" she purred, "you must Briggs". Briggs took her round the waist, snogged her and then smiled and cried a bit.

"Correct, lady" he barked and she purred. Louis was busy doingsomething boring. The sexual chemistry was so stron[g] between Briggs and Mary Hopkins that you could smell like a really strong smell, petrol for example.

"So you are the great Detective Briggs" she said and tossed her hair on the settee. "The great Detective [Briggs] who does things HIS way and gets results and als[o a] brilliant kisser."

"Correct again Sister" Briggs said. He'd suddenl[y] that Mary Hopkins was a nun. This would be a even for someone as handsome and attractive as

"And this" she said, smoothing her habit, "n police dog."

"No, that's PC Louis." Briggs snarled. "Louis get some statements. Also, make me some my other suit to the cleaners. Quick, or I'll I'm your Boss." Louis scurried outside nun back on the settee (the body had been take[n] now) and snogged her red lips.

"My, my you are in a hurry" she said, kissing him back dead hard.

"Life's short" Briggs said.

"So are you" said Mary Hopkins.

METROPOLITAN POLICE

MEMORANDUM

FROM: Detective Inspector Land (Drugs Squad)

TO: Superintendent Cottam (C Division)

RE: DC Briggs and DC Louis

Dear Frank,

I hardly feel it is worth putting pen to paper to gripe about the behaviour of your two 'Detectives' who were seconded to my unit at short notice last Saturday night. When I heard who we'd been sent, I feared the worst, but I must say their antics exceeded even my own pessimistic forecast. As you may have heard, we asked Briggs and Louis to work undercover for a few hours, posing as waiters. We wanted them to eavesdrop on a table where we thought a large drug shipment was being organized.

It seems that while they waited in the kitchens of the restaurant for our suspects to arrive, they discovered that the lobsters in the chilled cabinet were kept alive until cooking (standard restaurant practise). After several glasses of white wine, they became maudlin and sentimental about the fate of the lobsters, then angry. I won't bore you with the details of the radio conversations we had with them as they berated us about the unfortunate crustacea, but suffice it to say that by eight pm they had set off in a squad car, lights flashing, with two live lobsters under their coats. They drove all the way to Clacton, where they apparently set their little friends free in touching ceremony underneath the pier. I believe they both wrote 'good luck' messages on the lobsters' shells.

Frank, I've always been a philosophical sort of individual and I believe it takes all sorts to make a world. But perhaps, next time we need to ask you for a couple of 'fill ins' for a major operation, you could send us two detectives who don't have quite such a keen sense of injustice as regards shellfish.

Yours with amused contempt,

D. I. Land

DI Land.

Unbelievabl...
It gets wors...

with the compliments

INTERNAL AFFAIRS INTERVIEW TRANSCRIPT

TIME OF INTERVIEW; 12.15 August 1st 1995.

INTERVIEWEE; Frank Cottam.

RANK; Superintendent.

SUBJECT OF INTERVIEW; Briggs/Louis.

FILE No: IA 128

ANDREWS; As DC Briggs and DC Louis' cc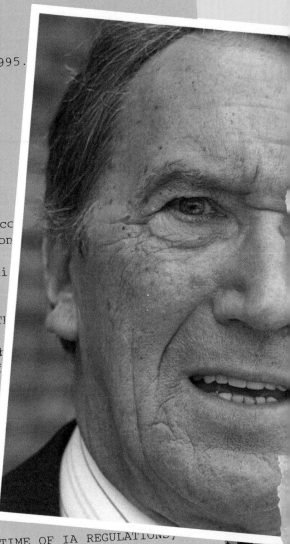
what is your general overall impression

COTTAM; Look, Terry, can't we have thi
record?

(INTERVIEWEE REMINDED THAT ALL IA INTI

COTTAM; OK, OK, if you're going to h
about this....They're....they're diff

ANDREWS; Different to what?

COTTAM; To everyone else.

ANDREWS; Be more specific.

COTTAM; How can I? Look, Terry,
Dog and Duck and sort this out ove

(INTERVIEWEE REMINDED FOR A SECOND TIME OF IA REGULATIONS)

COTTAM; OK, what can I tell you. They're hopeless,
helpless, hapless, useless. They've been a thorn in my
side ever since I took 'C' Division over. It's been like
being the father of two particularly large, difficult
children. I've lain awake at nights....I've spent hours
pacing the floor....for Christ's sake Terry you knew me in
the old days. I didn't look like this. I didn't drink
Scotch from the bottle. I was a pints and darts man. I
didn't have to wear this stupid wig, or take tranquilisers,
or listen to those special hypnotists tapes just so I could
get an erection....

ANDREWS; I beg your pardon?

COTTAM; Nothing. Terry, at least strike that last bit off the record....

ANDREWS; I can't. Carry on.

COTTAM; Yes, I admit it. They've made my life hard. I've been this close to jacking it all in a hundred times. Of course it hasn't all been Briggs and Louis' fault. I mean, Marjorie slinging her hook didn't help. Bloody Nat West bank. If I'd have known that all their bank clerks were ginger haired lotharios looking to run off with other people's wives I'd have gone to Barclays. At least they give you a plastic wallet and a book voucher.

ANDREWS; Superintendent, could we get back to....

COTTAM; I don't know what on earth she saw in him. He was half her age. Bastard.

ANDREWS; Superintendent...Frank....

COTTAM; Oh yes we can all go round wearing tight jeans and torn T-shirts, it doesn't make you a good husband does it? It doesn't mean you'll be there when times get tough. Who looked after her when her kidneys went? Eh? Who talked her down when she was up on the roof of Asda? Me, that's who. Muggins. Joe Muggins the Mug from Mugshire. Where was he when she had her hysterectomy, eh? In bloody primary school, that's where....

ANDREWS; Superintendent, I only want to talk to you about Briggs and Louis.

COTTAM; Briggs and Louis? What have they got to do with it? They didn't have an affair with my wife....

(INTERVIEWEE APPROACHES IN THREATENING MANNER)

...unless of course you know something I don't. Come on, out with it!

ANDREWS; Frank.....why don't we go down the Dog and Duck for a swift half?

COTTAM; Yeah. OK. Sorry mate.

March 2, 1975 ★ ★ ★ ★

Rugby Union

C DIVISION CRASH TO RECORD DEFEAT

E Division 205...C Division 0

C Division's first XV re-wrote the record books at the Hillside ground on Saturday when they conceded twenty-nine tries in a woefully one-sided encounter. E Division scored at will as they sliced through a new-look defence built around recent recruits Dave Briggs and Bob Louis.

Time and again Briggs and Louis were other 'C' Division players meant that cap-

The Dog

THURSDAY, MARCH 2, 1975

Witness Statement

MC Act 1980, s.102, M

....

insert 'over?

sign

Truncheon Polish.

The finest boiled and panfried Linseed Oil – a few strokes twice a day is sure to keep your baton firm.

Prevents woodworm, dry rot, wet rot and fungal

Rugby Probe Shock For Inter-Divisional Championship

each other as the ball came towards them. All too often, colleagues and supporters alike were treated to the sight of the new pairing crawling from beneath the ruck, obviously close to tears. Briggs' debut as goal-kicker was no more successful. On the few occasions he actually managed to propel the ball into the air he was forced to immediately leave the field complaining of sore ankles. His effective range, despite spending up to 20 minutes constructing "those little sandcastles you put the ball on" was no more than three yards.

Louis' interest in the game diminished from the moment, in the first minute of play, when he got mud on his hands. He also complained that he was too cold and that the ball was too hard. Injuries to

games". After the game, Wellings expressed his disappointment in the performance of his debutant players. "Briggs and Louis both assured me that they had played at County level. In fact Briggs claimed that he was forced to turn down a place in the England team to concentrate on his kick-boxing career. He said his place in the side was taken by Will Carling. And Brian Moore. And Rory Underwood. Louis said he had played for London Welsh, London Irish, London Scottish and London English. They were very convincing. I'm somewhat disillusioned. I think they might just have been doing it to impress our Club President, the Chief Superintendent."

Duty

	Time

Monday
Dec 18

Duty To Which Posted   9 am/~~pm~~ till 5 ~~am~~/pm

On ....
Off ....
Hours
Pay or Time ....

9am First job, which I have to do every Monday morning is sharpening the pencils because ~~Pete~~ D.C. Briggs won't do it, and in fact he's the one who's bitten all the little pink rubbers off the tops of them, and then chewed the ends. These pencils are now useful for one thing. i.e., if Dave is ever murdered by ~~Mr Manson~~ vicious gangland gangsters who cut off his ha

Tuesday
Dec 19

Duty To Which Posted   9 am/pm till 5 am/pm

On ....
Off ....
Hours
Pay or Time ....

9am Paperwork, paperwork and more ~~fire~~ paperwork! That's the bind with this job. Dave says that all this paperwork is interfering with our ability to do our jobs properly. He says we should be out on the streets catching criminals not wasting our time scratching away at pathetic bits of paper hoping that something turns up against the odds. He suggests that we should go to the bookies instead.

Wednesday
Dec 20th 10am

Duty To Which Posted   8 am/~~pm~~ till 13:30 am/pm

On ....
Off ....
Hours
Pay or Time ....

Woops! Sorry! late! Alarm didn't go off on my new Divers Alarm Chronograph. Must have set it wrong. Dave is v. jealous of it and is pretending it looks rediculous on me because its much wider than my wrist. He says it looks like a dustbin lid lying on a clothes line. (~~Bollock Brain~~)

Not much on, so we go to the pub ~~#~~ for a working lun

Thursday
Dec 21st.

Duty To Which Posted   10 ~~am~~/pm till 3 am/pm

On ....
Off ....
Hours
Pay or Time ....

Woken by loud clanging noise which turns out to be my deep sea divers watch ticking. I expect it's like that so you can hear it underwater.
But late reporting for duty due to inability to cross road because of fear of being run over. It is raining heavily and I got soaking wet. Note with some surprise that divers watch is FULL of water and hands have gone rusty. Go to see Reg in King's Arms.

M.P.87

Rank/Name D.G. Robert Louis

Duty	Reason Code	Claims	Mileage		Cash		Prisoners	
Time			Trip	C'tive	£	p	Arrests	Other Prisoners
			B/F					

and burn his clothes and leave his body naked and battered, face down in a water filled, disused quarry, then we'll be able to identify him from the dental records he has left all over the pencils. Not that I want this to happen. - Go to stores for new box of pencils, but have wrong sort of chit. Go to stationers in the High Street instead.

Claims: 1. Box of H.B. Pencils. — 3.95

1130 Lost £5 on a horse which I was certain would win because he had the same name as my Aunties bungalow in Redditch. Go to the Kings Arms instead for game of darts. Reg offers to sell me one of his watches. Buy proper diver's watch for just £15. It has many buttons and can go v. deep.

~~5·00~~ ~~15·00~~

am. Working lunch begins. - Kings Arms.

Working lunch ends.
5 Working tea starts - King's Arms.

30 (Approx, watch has stopped) Working tea ends.

Kings Arms. Reg seems unconcerned "You shouldn't have got it wet you prat" he says. Ha ha! Now I've got him "look at this" I said, showing him the back of the watch. "It says 'guaranteed to 200 meters'" "yeah" he sais "that means 200 meters from this pub." I am about to arrest him but Dave reminds me how much paperwork this will involve. Go home early.

Form 232

Totals: 3 95

	Time			
Friday	**Duty To Which Posted**			OFF Duty TODAY AT LAST
....		am/pm till	am/pm	
On				
Off			CHRISTMAS	
Hours				
Pay or Time				

	Duty To Which Posted	5 am/pm till	3 am/pm
Saturday Dec 23rd	The big day! The day of the station Christmas Party. Dave and I exchanged gifts before we went out. I got him a mucky video (nicked from Vice Squad office) and he got me a desk top pencil sharpener. At the party Dave and I were on the same table as Mounted Division. Honestly, what characters! We had a beer drinking competition where you had to drink a pint of beer as quickly as possible, then		
On			
Off			
Hours			
Pay or Time			

	Duty To Which Posted	am/pm till	am/pm
Sunday	'Tis the day before Christmas, And all threw' the nick Not a copper is moving, They're all being sick.		
....			
On			
Off			
Hours			
Pay or Time			

Continuation Space	who looked a bit like ferrets. I must say, she changed her tune a bit later on. I saw her kissing Nosher under the mistletoe, and he had stuck his piece (of mistletoe) into his flies. Women. Will we ever fully understand them? Christmas Day tomorrow. Looking forward to sharing a Bernard Matthews turkey breast at Dave's flat.

Duty		Claims		Mileage		Cash		Prisoners	
Time		Reason Code		Trip	Ctive	£	p	Arrests	Other Prisoners
				B/F					

SHOPPING

...everyone at the table who could ride a horse was allowed to punch anyone who couldn't. Dave and I were black and blue I can tell you! At about midnight Dave went off to tell the Chief Super how the division should be run. I, meanwhile, managed to corner W.Pc Broad lady under the Mistletoe. Unfortunately she said that she didn't believe in sexual relations between colleagues, Christmas or not, especially involving colleagues –

Misstletoe
(I hope)

| | | | Totals | | | 3 | 95 | | |

HO HO HO

Supervising Officer

Date

Weekly Summary	
Overtime Red	
Overtime Black	
Refreshment	
Travelling	
Incidental	3·95
Total	

The Complaints Department
Metropolitan Poilce
New Scotland Yard
St. James' Park
London SW1

26 July 1995

Dear Sir/Madam,

An official complaint has already been sent as regards the behaviour of certain officers during this year's Metropolitan Police Gala dinner. The breakdown of damages is as follows:

Broken wine glasses x 47
Broken plates/cups/misc china x 132
Broken banqueting tables x 2
Banqueting table damaged but repairable x 1
Broken chairs x 4
Broken chandelier (17th century) x 1
Broken store room door x 1
Stolen cleaning fluid/Windolene/Mr Muscle x 12 bottles/cans
Irreparably damaged silver service punch bowl and ladle x1
Broken fingers of head wine waiter x 2 (Plus badly bruised thumb)

The above list includes most of the damage caused during what was a truly regrettable evening. In brief, two officers broke open the door to the hotel stock cupboard, stole the cleaning fluid, Windolene and Mr Muscle and poured and sprayed it into the punch bowl, thus dissolving the antique silver bowl and ladle. After drinking the punch from the bowl, the same two officers were hoisted up to the ceiling by a human pyramid formed by the Met police motorcycle display team, where they both began to swing from the chandelier, claiming to be 'Shadow and Wolf out of the Gladiators'. When the inevitable happened and the chandelier gave way, they crashed twenty feet on to the three banqueting tables and chairs, thus smashing the tables, chairs, glasses, plates and misc china. I suppose in

The Imperial Hotel
Grosvenor Street London W1R 9XX Telephone 0171-672 8971 Fax 0171-672 0921
International Booking Code: Hot Imp Grov L

circumstances, the head wine waiter only has himself to blame for
ing to catch them as they fell. I did not manage to catch the names
the two officers who caused most of the trouble, but one was thin
d bald and looked like a ferret and the other was dark and
nbearably arrogant. When I tried to take their names at the time of
e incident the arrogant one told me, 'The trouble with you Italians
s, you don't know how to enjoy yourselves.' I might point out, for
what it's worth, that I am in fact from Malta and I do indeed know
how to enjoy myself. I sit with my family and enjoy an evening of
good food, fine wine and intelligent conversation. I do not drink
window cleaning fluid and do dangerous impressions of my
television heroes. I trust the bill of SEVEN THOUSAND TWO
HUNDRED AND TWENTY FIVE POUNDS which is now
outstanding will be paid without delay.

Yours with regret,

METROPOLITAN POLICE

ent **Andrews**
nternal Affairs

01/1-672 8971 Fax 0171-672 0921

Booking Code: Hot Imp Grov L

ty of the Metropolitan Police – Return to Central Records Office

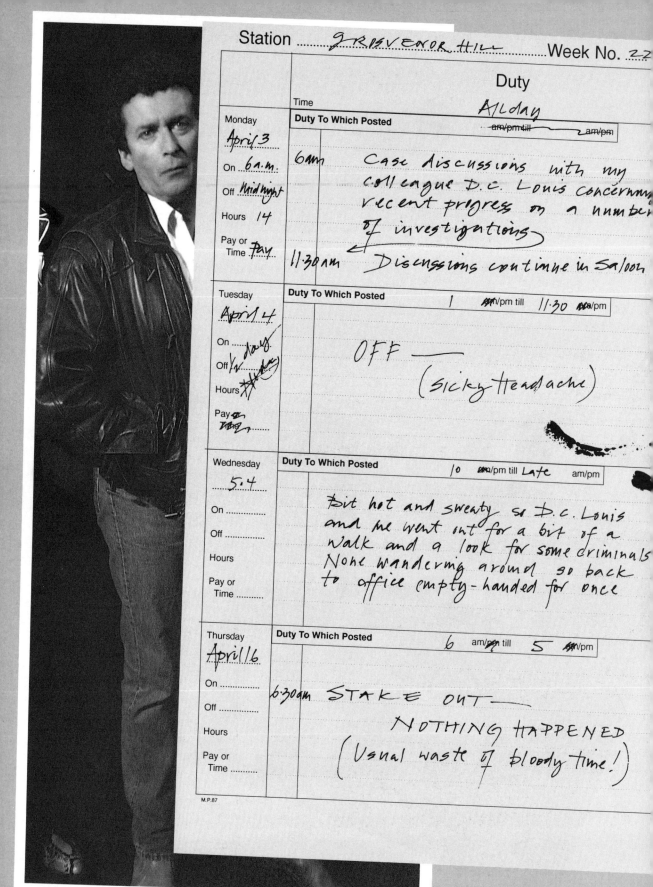

Station .... GROSVENOR HILL .... Week No. 22

Duty

	Time	Duty	
		All day	am/pm till ____ am/pm

Monday
April 3
On 6 a.m.
Off Midnight
Hours 14
Pay or Time Pay

Duty To Which Posted

6am   Case discussions with my colleague D.C. Louis concerning recent progress on a number of investigations

11.30am ← Discussions continue in Saloon

Tuesday
April 4
On ...... day
Off ......
Hours ~~X~~
Pay or ~~Time~~

Duty To Which Posted   1 am/pm till 11.30 am/pm

OFF —
(Sicky Headache)

Wednesday
5.4
On ....
Off ....
Hours
Pay or Time ....

Duty To Which Posted   10 am/pm till Late am/pm

Bit hot and sweaty so D.C. Louis and me went out for a bit of a walk and a look for some criminals. None wandering around so back to office empty-handed for once

Thursday
April 6
On ....
Off ....
Hours
Pay or Time ....

Duty To Which Posted   6 am/pm till 5 am/pm

6.30am STAKE OUT —
NOTHING HAPPENED
(Usual waste of bloody time!)

M.P.87

Rank/Name D.C. Briggs

Duty		Claims	Mileage		Cash		Prisoners	
Time	Reason Code		Trip	Ctive	£	p	Arrests	Other Prisoners
			B/F					

bar of King's Arms for reasons of confidentiality

3pm Conversation moves on to 1966 World Cup Final and Pamela Anderson out of Baywatch. Return to office

7pm Inter division darts match Kings Arms — Darts — 8 pints bitter crisps — — — 16 25 — Won! 4-0

7pm Meetings with underworld contacts. Pimps, drug addicts, fences, muggers, People like that

Venue: Kings Arms — 6 Pints bitter 3 Scotches Cheese sandwich — — — 17 75 — No actual arrests

LUNCH CANTEEN

* C. DIVISION SUBUTEO TOURNAMENT
SEMI FINALS
Briggs and Louis
v
Willis and Hargreaves

10pm Post match victory parade through car park to Kings Arms — * 4 pints bitter — — — 8 05

pm Still nothing happening. We pop to Co-op for some food Including: — Mileage — 22·00 — — — NIL

2 x Ginsters Pasties 1 x Scotch Egg
2 x Isotonic Sports Drinks, 4 Wagon wheels
bag of mini Baby-bells, 8 cans Kestrel,
Half bottle of Scotch (Expenses opposite) — Lunch — — — 27 36
Return to office. Utter, Utter, Utter waste of time

Form 282

| Totals | 22·00 | 69 | 36 |

Duty

	Time			
Friday April 17 On .... 7 a.m. Off .... Hours Pay or Time	**Duty To Which Posted**	7	~~till~~ #3 3	am/pm
	7am High-level meeting with Superintendent Cottam to discuss yesterday's stake-out operation, with particular reference to viz-a-vis matters arising from our disappearance to Co-op during period of alleged felons arrival at house. Full and 'frank' exchange of views. Most satisfactory			
Saturday .... On .... Off .... Hours Pay or Time	**Duty To Which Posted**		am/pm till	am/pm
	6 AM ~~GOLF WITH BOB~~ CANCELLED			
Sunday .... On .... Off .... Hours Pay or Time	**Duty To Which Posted**		am/pm till	am/pm
	OFF — THAN			
Continuation Space				

Duty		Claims		Mileage		Cash		Prisoners	
	Reason Code			Trip	Cttve	£	p	Arrests	Other Prisoners

Time
Noon. Meeting with Detective Constable Louis in King's Arms
re matters arising from this morning's
meeting with the super. Topics covered
included ① The difference between men and women
　　　② Friendship.
　　　③ Loyalty
　　　④ What we're all here for
　　　⑤ Whether or not the bloke in
　　　　the corner was looking at us
　　　　in a funny way
　　　⑥ Whether or not the barmaid
　　　　fancies me more than D.C. Louis
　　　⑦ Friendship (again)
　　　⑧ Nigel Mansell
　　　⑨ The future — Whither
　　　⑩ Cruelty to animals
The meeting continued later in
Ritzie's nightclub, where we discussed
what the Germans had done to Bob's dad
during the Last Lot

GOD

B/F — Trip 22 00 / £ 69 p 36 / Arrests 0 / Other 0

(circled) 0 0

Refreshments — 147 22

(circled) 0 0

| | | Totals | | 22 00 | | 216 58 | | 0 | 0 |

REFUSED

Supervising Officer
11.4.95 Date

Send Briggs to
see me F.G.

Weekly Summary	
Overtime Red	LOTS
Overtime Black	TONS
Refreshment	216.58
Travelling	22.00
Incidental	4.00
Total	242.58

WHAT'S GOING ON? These two appear to have somehow accessed their data files at central records and amended them somewhat. It would surely take a computer genius (or a child of eight) to get into their files, and a complete idiot to change them in the way they have. . .

METROPOLITAN POLICE

with the compliments of Chief Superintendent Andrews

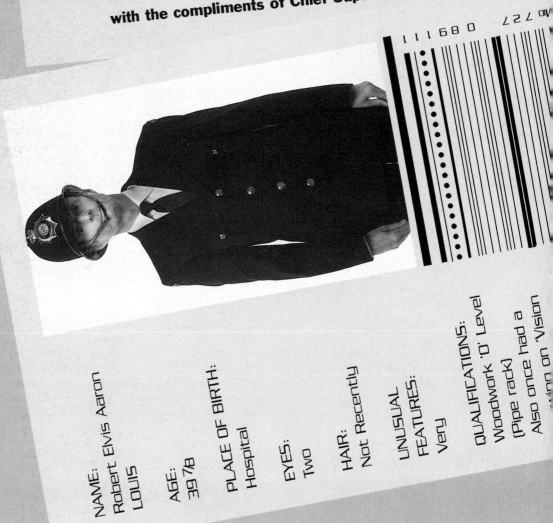

NAME:
Robert Elvis Aaron
LOUIS

AGE:
39⅞

PLACE OF BIRTH:
Hospital

EYES:
Two

HAIR:
Not Recently

UNUSUAL FEATURES:
Very

QUALIFICATIONS:
Woodwork 'O' Level
[Pipe rack]
Also once had a
____ing on 'Vision

NAME:
David Ian Lovelace
BRIGGS

AGE:
Won't say

PLACE OF BIRTH:
Manchester
(the posh bit)

EYES:
Penetrating

HAIR:
by Maurice

DISTINGUISHING ED
FEATURES:
Correct

QUALIFICATIONS:
19 'O' Levels
5 'A' Levels
B.A. PHD. MSc

COMMENTS:
Compulsive Liar
(see above)

RANK:
Chief
Superintendent

on to
one slip through

RANK:
Field
Marshal

A novel by David Briggs.

THE HARD MAN

CHAPTER 4

Inspector Briggs gunned the engine of his Porsche 911 Turbo and stroked the wheel, easily taking the dangerous, curvey mountain bend at one hundred and fifty miles an hour. "Oh Sir, Sir" whined Louis, cowering in the back seat. There isn't actually a back seat as such in the Porsche 911 but Louis had managed to squeeze himself onto that back shelf thing like a sort of pathetic Garfield.

"Oh Sir, Sir, don't go so fast" he whined again. "I don't like going at this speed because basically I'm a coward"

"Fast?" Briggs snarled, teasing the car round a hairpin, "this isn't fast. Fast is when you're doing three hundred in your Formula One Racing Car round the track at Monte Carlo, which I have done, many times. Fast is when you're hurtling back to earth in your space shuttle at about ten thousand miles an hour, which I have also done when I was part of the british space programme. Fast is when you are forced to take over the controls of Concorde on a transatlantic flight because the pilot has died and nobody else on the plane knows what all the buttons do, something which I have also done. Twice. Why twice? Don't ask. I guess me and danger go together like Pearl and Dean. But this ain't no picture show, Lady.

By the way, there was also a tall cool blonde on the back seat of the Porsche, or the 'back shelf', as I described earlier. Briggs wasn't calling Louis 'Lady', he was talking to her. She was one of his many girlfriends and he had just rescued her from an international gang of gold, jewels and drug thieves who had been torturing her to find out her secrets. Briggs had burst into their mountain top secret fortress, protected by hundreds of men in white overalls and got her out to safety. Louis had waited in the car, eating the sandwiches his Mother had made.

"You sure know how to handle a fast car" the tall cool blonde said, climbing into the passenger seat, virtually naked.

Inspector Briggs smiled and chewed a match and lit a

METROPOLITAN POLICE

A GUIDE TO PHYSICAL CONTAINMENT OF VIOLENT SUSPECT

1.

2.

3.

1. Politely address the suspect, warning him that you will use force if given no other option.

2. Inform him of his rights and try to make him see the error of his ways.

3. If needs be, apply gentle but firm physical means to assure him of your intentions. Keep calm. Avoid knee-jerk reactions.

4. Remember to keep talking. The stamp of authority is more readily impressed by means other than physical force.

4.

Officers of the Metropolitan Police are renowned for their ability to cope with potentially dangerous physical situations in a calm, composed and controlled manner. From the first day of their training, officers are, naturally, instructed to resort to physical means only if they themselves are threatened, or if they 'fancy a bit of a punch-up in the back of the van.' Restraint is a word that should be uppermost in every officer's thoughts. As opposed to *restraints,* which should only be used if you really want to give a suspect a good shoeing without the possibility of sustaining collateral injury. The photographs below illustrate the correct use of minimum force to subdue an adversary.

6.

5.

5. Once he is subdued and calm, offer the suspect a seat. You will assert a stronger physical presence standing over him.

6. Remember the drill. Force must at all times be kept to the minimum.

7. Keep a tight rein on the suspect. It is all too easy to relax your grip and offer escape opportunities.

8. Whatever you do, don't lose your head. Execute your duties, and your prisoner, with the professionalism expected of an officer of the Met. Happy hunting!

7. **8.**

INTERNAL AFFAIRS INTERVIEW TRANSCRIPT

TIME OF INTERVIEW; 4.50 July 21st.

INTERVIEWEE; Joanne Carson.

RANK; PC.

SUBJECT OF INTERVIEW; Briggs/Louis.

FILE No: IA 125.

ANDREWS; What is your overall, general impression of Briggs and Louis?

CARSON; Sweeties.

ANDREWS; Meaning?

CARSON; They're nice. Not like most of the blokes in the Division.

ANDREWS; In what way are they different?

CARSON; Sexually. I mean, they're not just interested in one thing like the others. Actually that's not true. They are interested, they just don't know what to do about it.

ANDREWS; But how are they as functioning members of the division?

CARSON; Oh, utterly useless. But they're so sweet you can't get angry with them. They're like two little soft fluffy puppies. I once came out with it and asked Louis if he was a virgin. He went all red and and said 'not yet'. Sweeeeeeet.

Sweeeeeeeet!!!! ??????
I call it bloody pathetic!!!!!

METROPOLITAN POLICE

perintendent Andrews
Internal Affairs

WPC JOANNE CARSON

Property of the Metropolitan Police – Return to Central Records Office

METROPOLITAN POLICE

MEMORANDUM

FROM: DI Kean, West Yorkshire Constabulary

TO: Superintendent Frank Cottam,
'C' Division, Metropolitan Police

Dear Superintendent Cottam,

This has been a trying couple of months for all of us. What with questions being raised about the police force's 'political role' and suggestions of the formulation of a national police force, it has been incumbent on all of us to protect the good name of serving officers. As I'm sure you know, there has been some controversy regarding the actions of members of the Metropolitan police force in particular. As well as the normal 'North/South' resentment, there have been accusations of heavy handedness and intimidation. However, I write to you with a complaint about two of your officers which completely flies in the face of these accusations. Their names are PC Briggs and PC Louis and their behaviour during the course of the disturbances was bizarre to say the least. As far as I can establish, Briggs and Louis arrived at Orgreave pit village along with two dozen other Metropolitan police officers and were billeted in a local school. For reasons unknown, the other officers were not prepared to have PCs Briggs and Louis sleeping in the billet with them. I gather it was something to do with smelly feet and snoring. After being ejected from the billet, Briggs and Louis began to wander around Orgreave pit village on the night before the real disturbances began. At around seven pm they entered the Orgreave Miners CIU social club and began to drink with some of the local miners. A laudable attempt to forge friendships across the divide, you might think. Sadly it went further than that.

After seven hours of heavy drinking (both beer and spirits I am told) PCs Briggs and Louis apparently began to see the justice of the miners' case. By midnight they were on stage at the social club, leading choruses of 'The Internationale' and 'You don't get me I'm part of the Union'. When some of the miners attempted to leave the club at two am Briggs and Louis hurled insults at them, accusing them of being 'class traitors'. By dawn, Briggs and

MEMORANDUM
Continued

METROPOLITAN POLICE

Louis had barricaded the social club doors with fruit machines, and were issuing 'communiques' to the 'running pigs of the capitalist media', suggesting that the entire strike was being financed by Imperialist American financiers, that Margaret Thatcher was Adolf Eichmann in drag, and that (bizarrely) all cruelty to little wittle pit ponies be banned forthwith. Sometime after eight, they burst forth from the social club with a rag tag army of equally drunk miners, armed with petrol soaked bags of scratchings and sharpened chair legs. When the initially peaceful stand off between pickets and police occurred, it was Briggs and Louis who led the charge towards the police lines, yelling 'Banzai', 'Death to the fascist goon squads' and 'Birmingham City for the Cup'. Is there some sort of undercover operation going on that I know nothing about? Are they agent provocateurs? When I asked them they they didn't seem to know what 'agent provocateur' meant. (Mind you, they were very hungover by then)

If Briggs and Louis are members of some elite, crack squad of undercover operatives then I really do think that I should have been told in advance. If, as I suspect, they are simply insane, then they should be disciplined forthwith. I do not enjoy being called a 'Nazi pig imperialist flunky' to my face by fellow officers. Nazi pig I may be, but I'm nobody's flunky.

Yours with deep concern,

Best Man's Speech for Nosher's Wedding.

*Don't forget RING! *

METROPOLITAN POLICE

Page 1.

Metropolitan Police Service

REPORT BOOK

Incident: *Dearly beloved, it is indeed a truly great privilege to be addressing you on the occasion of the wedding of the man we at 'C' Division all call Nosher. And it*

Arrest: *is a truly pleasant surprise that once again, he has managed to land himself a bride with such obvious charms. Some of you here may remember Nosher's previous wedding when he married that ~~tart~~ girl (check name of 1st wife) who was, of ~~course, a bit younger than this one,~~ but may I say, a lot less showy in her outfit. Some of you who were at that first wedding ~~may even remember~~ this suit I'm wearing with the humorous 'bottomless' pockets, and of course this bowtie....*

* FLASH THE TIE ON AND OFF. CHECK BATTERIES! *

It is traditional of course for the best man to tell some ~~humorous anecdotes about the Groom's past. Sadly I didn't~~ know Nosh as a young man, but in the time I've known him, he ~~has certainly done some humorous things. Once, when the~~ coffee machine ran out of water, he punched it and said 'Why ~~is there never any water in this bloody machine?'~~ Another time, he wore his cap backwards. ~~On another memorable occasion, in a nightclub in Reading, he tried to get a girl ratarsed drunk~~ in order that he could ~~fuck~~ sleep ~~with~~ with her!
* WAGGISH WINK TO BRIDE)

Officer reporting _____ Rank _____ No _____
Warrant No_____
Area/Div code_____ Branch _____

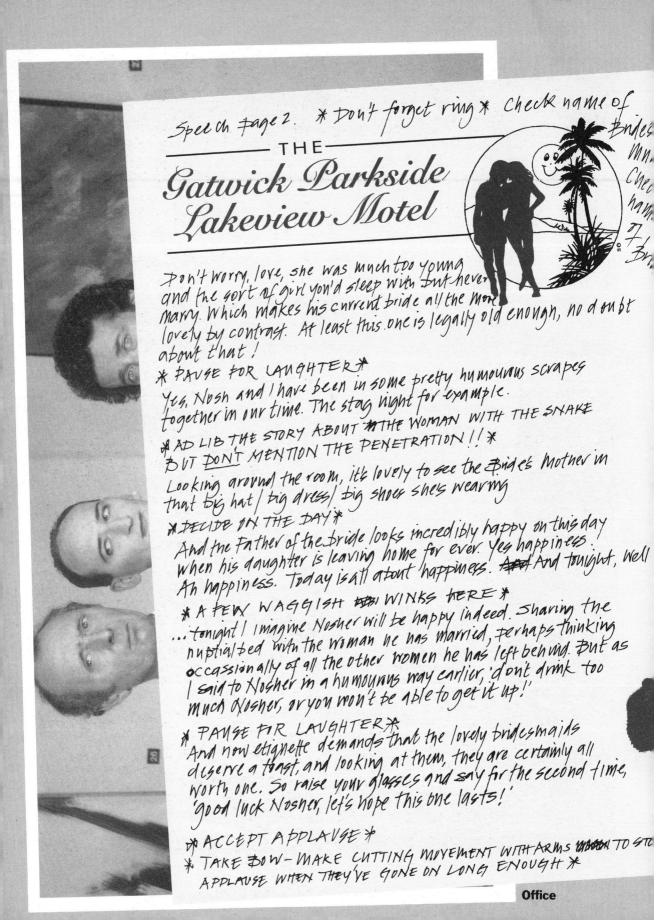

THE
Gatwick Parkside Lakeview Motel

Don't worry, love, she was much too young and the sort of girl you'd sleep with but never marry. Which makes his current bride all the more lovely by contrast. At least this one is legally old enough, no doubt about that!

* PAUSE FOR LAUGHTER *

Yes, Nosh and I have been in some pretty humourous scrapes together in our time. The stag night for example.

* AD LIB THE STORY ABOUT THE WOMAN WITH THE SNAKE BUT DON'T MENTION THE PENETRATION !! *

Looking around the room, it's lovely to see the Bride's Mother in that big hat / big dress / big shoes she's wearing

* DECIDE ON THE DAY *

And the Father of the Bride looks incredibly happy on this day when his daughter is leaving home for ever. Yes happiness. Ah happiness. Today is all about happiness. And tonight, Well

* A FEW WAGGISH WINKS HERE *

...tonight I imagine Nosher will be happy indeed. Sharing the nuptial bed with the woman he has married, perhaps thinking occasionally of all the other women he has left behind. But as I said to Nosher in a humourous way earlier, 'don't drink too much Nosher, or you won't be able to get it up!'

* PAUSE FOR LAUGHTER *

And now etiquette demands that the lovely bridesmaids deserve a toast, and looking at them, they are certainly all worth one. So raise your glasses and say for the second time, 'good luck Nosher, let's hope this one lasts!'

* ACCEPT APPLAUSE *
* TAKE BOW - MAKE CUTTING MOVEMENT WITH ARMS TO STO
   APPLAUSE WHEN THEY'VE GONE ON LONG ENOUGH *

Why Drugs Are
Bad For You

D.C. David Briggs

WHY DRUGS ARE BAD FOR YOU

The marijuana joint or *spliff*. Just one innocent puff and you can be hooked for life, drawn ever deeper into a degrading downward spiral of filth, squalor, dirty hands and general unpleasantness.

This joint or *reefer* is being smoked by a volunteer under carefully-controlled laboratory conditions to demonstrate the evil effects of this vile contaminant.

● The joint or *electric wand* is ignited. Initial effects are not unpleasant. The soon-to-be addict will experience a mild high. This may manifest itself as a fluttery feeling in the tummy, similar to that experienced when left alone in the garden shed with several back-issues of *Razzle*.

● Euphoria increases. This is when the drug-fiend experiences *the buzz*. Suddenly, everything seems screamingly funny, like when you're at the funeral of a close relative. Motes of dust, tears in the wallpaper, the contents of the fridge - yes, even ITV sitcoms - can suddenly appear terribly amusing.

● The addict hits *the wall*. It's downhill from here I'm afraid. A wave of nausea engulfs the victim as microscopic hydroprotonutrins actually contained *within* the carcinophins penetrate the receptor nodes at the back of larynctal privet hedge.

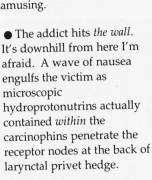

I ask you. Whatever next???

● Uh-oh. Now our guinea-pig feels sick as a parrot. Or our parrot feels sick as a guinea-pig. One or the other. Anyway, the victim is now covered in pustulating acne, has grown a pathetically wispy goatee beard and may find that his trousers have flared irrevocably at the ankle.

● Under the volcano. Weird figures swim out of the walls chanting and slavering and mucking around with their testicles and everything is covered in paisley. The victim will fall prey to delusions of paranoia, schizophrenia and quadrophenia. Hundreds of bats will appear, speaking Spanish, and the addict will start to dance in a drippy fashion. In extreme cases, he may hallucinate so powerfully that he begins to believe that Oasis are both good *and* original.

● Cold turkey. Thousands of tiny imps in slingback stilettos lambada across the victim's flesh, prodding his privates with crochet needles and inserting organic vegetables into his fundament. On the down side the addict will feel jolly thirsty and ever so peckish. He is hooked. His life is no longer his own. He is doomed to the black abyss of hell or, even worse, sharing a squat in Hackney with other drug-crazed hippies getting all arsey about whose turn it is to do the washing-up.

Remember kids. Don't do it!

Form A/a 421

ACCIDENT REPORT

Date: 28 / 7 / 95

METROPOLITAN POLICE

VEHICLE(S) INVOLVED: Unmarked Vauxhall Omega.
Civilian Hearse.

OFFICER(S) INVOLVED: D.C. Louis

DATE OF INCIDENT: 24 July 1995

OFFICER'S ACCOUNT:
I was proceeding along the A40 in hot pursuit of
~~a stolen vehicle. I left the A40 to take a short~~
cut to 'cut him off at the pass' as they say in
old films about cowboys. In doing so, I came
~~into contact with one of them big black hearses.~~
I hit it up the back end, not realizing that it
~~was going slow. It was going slow because there~~
was some funny looking bloke in a black hat
walking in the middle of the road in front of it.
~~There was substantial damage to the~~ ~~Cosworth~~ OMEGA but
the hearse only sustained a damaged rear door.
Using my special powers (Section B4, vehicle and
Highways) I comandeered the black car and
continued my hot pursuit. Two miles down the
~~A40, the coffin flew out of the damaged rear door~~
and the coffin broke open. Not wishing to leave
the deceased on the carriageway, I put him in the
~~passenger seat and continued towards Reading~~
intending to return him to his loved ones when I
~~had caught the 'baddies'. I imagine that hearses~~
are unaccustomed to high speeds, and somewhere
around High Wycombe, it burst into flames and hit
~~the central reservation. I was suddenly~~
unconscious, and woke to find an AA man giving my
~~dead passenger the kiss of life. When I~~
explained to him that he had been dead long
before the accident I was rushed to hospital with
~~suspected concussion. I was later told that my~~
dead friend was also rushed to hospital and
declared dead for the second time in his life,
~~which might be something of a first.~~

Motor pool verification:

Verification Officer: E. Bilko

POST CARD

Dear all at 'C' Division
We have been drinking for four days
without a break. The first two days we
drank beer but we both came out in
rashes like hundreds of nipples on our
upper bodies so we switched to wine.
The rash is gone but our teeth have
gone black. No luck with the totty (they
seem to be scared of our teeth) but we
did win a darts match against some
muslim women. I havent produced
anything solid in the toilet for 3 days.
It must be something I've eaten.

All the best,
Bob (Louis) (as if you didn't know)
        P.S. I hope somebody is feeding my mouse.

All at 'C' Division,

'The Nick'

Crematorium Road,

London, WC2

Angleterrèè

Gibraltar – Where life ends up on the Rocks

POST CARD

Dear all at 'C' Division,
Gibraltar is truly breathtaking. The
panoramic views from the ⬛ top of
the 'Rock' took me back to my days
hiking in the Cairngorms. What a
delight it is to stroll through the ancient
ramparts of the Moorish castles,
converse in fluent Gibraltese with the
wrinkly old fisherfolk, share a bottle of
good honest rough suncountry wine with
the humble goat herds and monkey
wranglers who are always happy to
share their simple repast. Ah yes,
Robert and I have truly discovered the
meaning of the word 'foreign culture'.
Adios amigos,
David.

P.S. Get hold of a mouse skeleton and put it in the cage so Bob
thinks his mouse is dead!

All at 'C' Division
'The Nick'
Crematorium Road,
London, WC2
Ingleterre

Gibraltar – Who gives a Monkey's?

MEMORANDUM

FROM: Superintendent ~~xxxxxxxxxxxxxxx~~ Cottam

TO: ~~xD.~~ ~~C~~ ~~xBriggsXXXX~~

RE: ~~xxxxxxxx~~ Timewasting

METROPOLITAN POLICE

'Tough Guy on Mean Streets'   A navel by David briggs

CHAPTER 14

'Cha shian Chiu' said Inspector Briggs in fluent Vietnamese. TheVietnamese waiter smiled and said something back in Vietnamese very fast which was a joke and Briggs laughed and winked at him."Good joke" he said, and all the other people at the table, four girls who looked like the girls in the Robert Palmer video, were impressed.

"So you speak Vietnamese" said one of the girls, putting on lipstick.

"Yeah" snarled Briggs and a smile played on his lips that turned quickly into a look of anger and fear and then turned back into a smile. He'd just had a flashback to Vietnam where he won loads of medals for running up to a machine gun nest with a red hanky round his head. He'd also flown choppers and saved babies from crocodiles.

"He won loads of medals" said a man sitting at another table who happened to know who Briggs was, so the girls knew about it without Briggs having to boast. Briggs tossed back his head and laughed and then went sad.

"I never talk about 'Nam" he growled, "come on girls, let's shoot through and get out of this turkey ranch and go grab ourselves some beer and have a bit of a dance.

"Briggs suddenly stood up, throwing his coat over his shoulder, throwing loads of money to the waiter and brushing back his long blond hair. The girls stood up as well and followed him. These girls by the way were trainee detectives who were following Briggs around so he could show them how to be detectives. They'd been told in advance that he was good....very good. They'd been told by the Super that he was good at fighting but nice, an expert marksman, an acrobat, a tireless charity worker and a bit of a card in the trouser department. They all fancied him like mad.

Anyway, they got to one of them discos that refuse to let people in if they're not trendy enough. But when the doorman saw Briggs, he greeted him in fluent Maori and Briggs answered him in Maori as well, doing the Maori greeting dance which can look a bit daft but in Briggs's case looked sexy.

"Come on girls" he said and they were all let in while everybody else in the queue looked at him and said to each other 'God he must be important'. "And good at sex judging by the women he's with' said another trendy man. 'You can tell that just by looking at him' said a girl in tight trousers. Briggs suddenly went 'Uuuuuugh!' because he'd had another flashback to Vietnam. Briggs was wearing his best clothes. His black suit with a ickie bow, the trousers that don't make him look fat, and shiny shoes and his shirt had a white ruffley thing down the front. He also had a sun tan from his mission to Bosnia. When he walked in, all the girls looked at him and went 'God, look at him.' Briggs smiled, ordered massive cocktails in Indonesian and

EMORANDUM

METROPOLITAN POLICE

ROM: Superintendent Cottam

O: DXC Briggs XXXXX

E: Expense claims

...hen went on to the dance floor. The record that was playing was the one ...with the line in it 'I wonder why, Mwaaaaaaa...he's the greatest dancer'.... ...nd Briggs began to gyrate his hips with one arm up in the air and one just ...bove his willy pants belt buckle.

Soon he was surrounded by a semi circle of fabulous women, and all the ...lokes were standing at the bar saying 'fair enough, my missus fancies him, ...ut who wouldn't, and anyway, if I start anything he'll beat me up.'

Just then a pathetic, spindly bald twat walked into the disco and everyone ...thought, 'how did he get in here?' Briggs saw that it was Louis in his pac a mac and bike clips and useless trousers.

"Sir, Sir" Louis whined, "I've got a message for you from the Super. He says it's urgent."

Briggs did another back flip over a pyramid of champagne glasses and landed like a cat behind Louis, who smelt of cheese and onion crisps.

"What's the message errand boy?" Briggs said, twirling around to the music.

"It's another big dangerous job. The Super said no one can handle it except you".Briggs laughed, tossed back his head, kissed the four trainee detective girls hard on the lips and grabbed his jacket.

"Catch ya later chicks" he said, and he did a sexy Rumb...

the door....

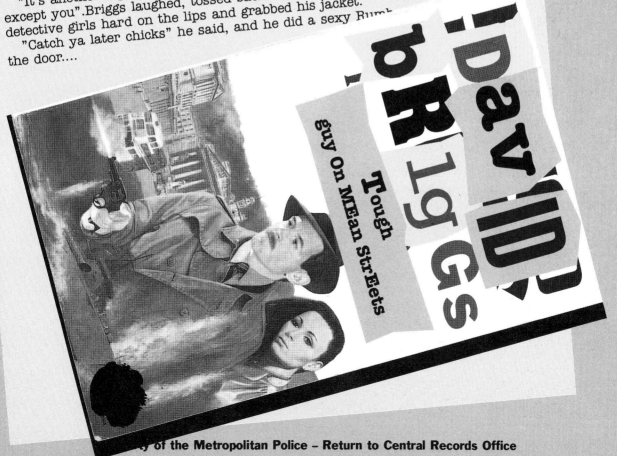

!DaVID bRIGGs

Tough On Mean StrEets

guy On Mean StrEets

INTERNAL AFFAIRS
Case Notes

Case No: 4727

File No: 704367

RE: Undercover work

Subject: Briggs and Louis

METROPOLITAN POLICE

IN THE SUMMER OF THIS YEAR, BRIGGS AND LOUIS WERE AT A LOOSE END. SUPERINTENDENT COTTAM GAVE THEM A PILE OF UNRESOLVED, NON-URGENT CASE FILES AND SUGGESTED THAT THEY PICK ONE AND GET ON WITH IT. ON JULY 14th, DC BRIGGS AND DC LOUIS DECIDED TO REOPEN THE INVESTIGATION INTO THE SUNSET MASSAGE PARLOUR IN COPLEY STREET. THEY ENTERED THE ESTABLISHMENT WEARING ONE-WAY AUDIO MICROPHONES CONCEALED BENEATH THEIR SHIRTS. THEIR BRIEF WAS TO ESTABLISH THAT THE YOUNG THAI MASSEUSES WERE OFFERING CLIENTS 'EXTRA SERVICES' ALONG WITH CONVENTIONAL MASSAGES. THE FOLLOWING IS A TRANSCRIPT OF THE AUDIO TAPE WHICH THEY RECORDED WHILE 'UNDERCOVER'...

3.15. BRIGGS AND LOUIS ENTER THE PARLOUR DRESSED AS BUSINESSMEN. THEY ARE GREETED BY THE RECEPTIONIST.

BRIGGS; Hello young lady. . . we'd like a microphone.

LOUIS; Massage!

RECEPTIONIST; I beg your pardon?

BRIGGS; We want a massage. Two massages. One each.

RECEPTIONIST; I thought you said microphone.

BRIGGS; No. No microphone.

LOUIS; He definitely said massage. The last thing we want is a microphone. We've got microphones.

BRIGGS; No we haven't.

LOUIS; No! We haven't got microphones.

BRIGGS; All talk of us having microphones is patently absurd. We are simply two weary businessmen down from Birmingham looking for a nice relaxing massage. No strings attached.

LOUIS; Nor wires.

BRIGGS; Exactly.

RECEPTIONIST; Well, what sort of massage would you like?

BRIGGS; Oh, you know.....

LOUIS; The full oriental style golfing holiday tired businessmen sort of massage.

Page 1

INTERNAL AFFAIRS
Case Notes

Case No: 4727

File No: 704367

RE: Undercover work

Subject: Briggs and Louis

METROPOLITAN POLICE

INTERNAL AFFAIRS
Case Notes

Case No: 4727   File No: 704367

RE: Undercover work

Subject: Briggs and Louis

**METROPOLITAN
POLICE**

RECEPTIONIST; You mean you'd like a Shiatsu.

LONG PAUSE.

LOUIS; That's a dog isn't it?

RECEPTIONIST; No, it is a Japanese massage technique which concentrates on stimulating the body's meridians. Are you experiencing any stiffness?

LOUIS; Not yet.

RECEPTIONIST; Tightness in the upper body? Twinges in the neck?

BRIGGS; Actually, now you come to mention it, I've been a martyr to my neck for a couple of months. I've tried Deep Heat but that stings and makes you smell old, doesn't it ?

RECEPTIONIST; Then perhaps you'd be interested in our physiotherapy massage.

BRIGGS; What, do you reckon that would help?

RECEPTIONIST; It's very good for Repetitive Stress Injury, you know, injuries sustained at work. Do you use a keyboard?

BRIGGS; As a matter of fact, Doctor, I do. I use a keyboard when I'm typing up arrest sheets. I only use one finger of course but. . . what did I say just then? Did I say arrest sheets? I did didn't I? Honestly, these tablets I'm taking. The chemist did say that one of the peculiar side effects of these tablets which I'm taking is that I would suddenly begin to imagine that I was a policeman. Funny isn't it, modern medication? I've been like it all day. Suddenly stopping people in the street saying, 'Come on son, you're nicked.' Daft! Mad!

RECEPTIONIST; You're on medication?

BRIGGS; Special pills. 'Warning,' it says, 'do not operate heavy machinery, do not be surprised if you suddenly start going around in big vans with numbers on the roof arresting people.'

RECEPTIONIST; Well, if you're on medication then maybe a massage isn't such a good idea.

PAUSE.

Page 3

INTERNAL AFFAIRS
Case Notes

METROPOLITAN POLICE

Case No: 4727   File No: 704367

RE: Undercover work

Subject: Briggs and Louis

LOUIS; I'm not! I'm not taking tablets. I'm a businessman and I know that's what I am and I don't spend any time at all thinking otherwise. That's what I am and I'm here now and I'd like a massage with a bit of rumpy pumpy thrown in.

RECEPTIONIST; Rumpy pumpy?

LOUIS; You know. . . rub and tug, executive extras, fat blokes playing golf, Bangkok, Madam Palm and her five lovely daughters.

RECEPTIONIST; Are you sure you're not on medication?

LOUIS; Come on love, you know the score.

RECEPTIONIST; Do you have something in your eye?

LOUIS; Look, we just want a rub down with a fluffy towel and a quick wa.....

THE PHONE RINGS.

RECEPTIONIST; Hello, Neale Road Alternative Healing Centre how can I help you?

PAUSE.

BRIGGS; Excuse me, love.

RECEPTIONIST; I'm on the phone...

BRIGGS; Did you just say 'Neale Road Alternative Healing Centre'?

RECEPTIONIST; I did.

LOUIS; Not the Sunset Executive Massage Emporium?

RECEPTIONIST; Oh goodness no, that closed down months ago. The police raided the place in July. Apparently the place was little more than a brothel.

LOUIS; Ah.

BRIGGS; I see....

RECEPTIONIST; Where are you going?

LOUIS; We must have picked up the wrong pile.....

RECORDING ENDS.

Page 4

METROPOLITAN POLICE

MEMORANDUM

FROM: Chief Superintendent Ken Burrows

TO: Superintendent FrankCottam

DATE: 6 March 1987

RE: The Usual

Frank,

I'm getting all kinds of flak from the brass at the Yard. Apparently no-one up there knew a thing about this Buzzy Bee bollocks – it was all their own work. The tragic thing is that they nearly got away with it. The Commissioner was highly impressed with the coverage, instilling public confidence, taking the fight against crime to the criminal and all that rubbish. If they hadn't moved on to shorts and got into a slanging match with that smart-arse from the *Independent* they'd be the heroes of the hour. I dread to think what's going to happen when he gets out of hospital. Try to drum it into them Frank: whatever they do, they must never again use their own initiative, or we're all for the high jump.

Ken

CHIEF SUPERINTENDENT BURROWS

P.S. Is Margaret back with you yet? Or is she still away? Hope things get back to normal soon.

INITIATIVE

BIZZIE'S BUZZY BEE BOUNTY

BY ROBIN BANKS – CRIME CORRESPONDENT

POLICEMEN IN LONDON are celebrating the success of a major crackdown on organised crime. Operation Buzzy Bee has been described as a "powerful blow against the crime community", "a rabbit punch in the kidneys for villainy" and "a kick in the bollocks for baddies" by officers behind the scheme. Speaking at a press conference held at the King's Arms public house in Wignall Street, Detective Constable Briggs – one of the two officers heading investigations – said Buzzy Bee sent out a clear message to criminals in the capital. "What Buzzy Bee is saying is this," he said, "It is saying it loudly, it is saying it clearly, and it is saying it over and over again. Sometimes it isn't just saying it it is shouting it, and on other occasions it is being whispered, or said through a megaphone. But by golly, whatever is being said is being received loud and clear by the few bad apples who – as the young Michael Jackson once observed – can spoil the whole bunch girl. We shall not give in to the powers of evil. By God we shall not. Never. Do you hear me? Never." DC Briggs' colleague, Bob Louis, agreed with the sentiment but pointed out that he'd thought up the name for the operation. "Thinking up the name for the operation is the most difficult bit really," said the exhausted but

Detectives Briggs and Louis proudly display the treasures recovered during Operation Buzzy Bee.

jubilant Detective Constable. "All the best ones – like Thrust, or Hammer, or Rapier - have already been used so it took me ages. In the end I got it from the song by the late, great Arthur Askey, a great man and a great performer. You know the one: 'I'm as busy as a busy little bee, busy buzz, busy buzz." The two officers proudly displayed the haul of potentially stolen goods recovered during the two-hour blitz, and invited Londoners to

come forward to reclaim their prized possessions. DC Briggs was unwilling to put a precise value on the recovered property but hinted that it could well be worth "many pounds". Scotland Yard's press office, meanwhile, said that they had no knowledge of Operation Buzzy Bee or of the authority of the two Detective Constables involved. Puzzled senior officers at the Yard are said to be looking into the case as a matter of some urgency.

HENDON CADET TRAINING COLLEGE

COURSE TUTOR'S REPORT

March 12 1970

METROPOLITAN POLICE

CADET NAME: Robert Elvis Aaron Louis

BASIC SKILLS ASSESSMENT
ATTITUDE AND APPROACH: 1/10.

One of the saddest cases I have ever encountered. The single mark awarded to him in this category is testament to his misplaced enthusiasm for the work – work for which, sadly, he displays no aptitude whatsoever. He has expressed ambitions of becoming a plain clothes detective. When pressed for his reasons he explained that he's always wanted "one of those big magnifying glasses" and that he finds the uniform trousers "a bit itchy"

PROCEDURE: 0/10.

Utterly beyond him, frankly. He seems to be doing his best, and spends hours staring at the textbooks with his tongue hanging out, but he has been on the same page since November, complaining that the set texts are "a bit short on pictures". His answer to a question in last week's modular tests (Q: How would you define a long criminal record? A: "The latest LP by Chicory Tip") graphically illustrates the limits of his abilities.

APPEARANCE: 0/10.

Has proved a real challenge to the lads in stores due to his complete lack of musculature. The equipment office had to make up a special pair of miniature handcuffs because standard issue pairs constantly slipped off his pathetically thin wrists, and armaments had to come up with a custom made truncheon - based on a ladies' badminton racquet - because his hands were too small to hold a normal one. His legs are so weedy that when his trousers flap in the breeze he looks like Douglas Bader, and his tortoisey neck swims around inside even the infants school-issue shirt (size 10) he wears, like a nodding dog in the back of a car. He is one of those people who manages to make the newest and smartest uniform look like Patrick Moore's gardening clothes, he smells like a trawlerman's vest, gets followed by feral cats and winos offer him swigs of their VP. All in all, not overly impressive.

Page 1

HENDON CADET TRAINING COLLEGE

How about putting him with that chap Biggs? Together I think they'd constitute a pretty fearsome crime-fighting team. At least, that's what God tells me. And after all, he knows everything.

Chief Superintendent Anderton
Head of Training

LEGE

CADET NAME: Robert Elvis Aaron Louis

PHYSICAL FITNESS: 0/10.

The problem is as above. As P.T. Sergeant McManus commented, "His chest looks like a thin strip of mouldy suet stretched over a toast rack." The basic forward roll is beyond him due to his inability to get his own mat off the pile without bursting into tears. When helped to the top of the wallbars his nose always starts bleeding and in one embarrassing incident, the fire brigade had to call upon the services of the Samaritans to talk him down. Plus he has the sort of pathetically narrow chest which means that his nipples are virtually on his back and his shoulder blades stick out so far that in profile he looks like a Christmas tree decoration. In short, hopeless.

SUMMARY:

This is the lowest score achieved since the Divisional Goat sat his sergeant's exams - and even he scored more on personal appearance and hygiene. And interpretation of regulations. That said, Monty the Goat has gone on to perform an extremely useful and productive role in the force and currently enjoys one of the highest arrest and conviction records in the entire vice squad. With the correct training and grooming, there is no reason why Louis should not emulate that success of Monty - and make less of a mess on the canteen floor. To exploit his potential to the full he should be placed with a responsible and capable junior officer.

F.R. Wainwright.

F R WAINWRIGHT COURSE TUTOR

Page 2

NATIONAL FOOTBALL INTELLIGENCE UNIT

SURVEILLANCE REPORT

DATE: April 14 1993

RE: Operation Cantona

*On Saturday May 12, myself and fellow officers
undercover unit were in position for covert mob
surveillance of crowds arriving for the FA Cup F
between Everton and Manchester United. We
advance warning that elements among both su
supporters might be gearing up for confrontatio...
the importance of the event and the potential for disc
Detectives Briggs and Louis were co-opted to Opera
Cantona with orders to mingle with supporters and in
trouble-makers. The timetable of the day - based up
observations (see attached photographs) - is as follo*

Noon: In position. Early arrivers making their way
peacefully towards the stadium. Briggs and Louis
identified among them, maintaining discreet surveilla

12.10pm: Briggs enters Manzo's 24-hour food ma
off-licence. Emerges with two cans Strongbow and
of Quavers. Surveillance maintained.

12.15pm: Louis enters Manzo's. Returns with eight cans
of pale ale and some Walnut Whips. Briggs and Louis
consume food and drink. They exchange good-natured
banter with arriving fans of both teams.

12.30pm: Larger numbers of fans arriving. Atmosphere
extremely peaceful. Rival fans shaking hands, swapping
scarves etc. Many family groups enjoying day out. Briggs
and Louis signal need to visit a lavatory.

12.32pm: Briggs and Louis enter the Malt Shovel public
house.

12.33-2.15pm: Large but good-humoured crowds in vicinity of the stadium. Community singing among fans. Manchester and Everton supporters exchanging shirts and other favours, swapping addresses and promising to keep in touch etc. Fans hand ticket tout over to uniformed officers. One arrest. Surveillance team prepares to stand down.

vel, arm-
rge
and
ren
e him.
attack

fficer

of

s
s

2
es
ca
pl
are
Arn

2.15pm: Briggs and Louis emerge from Malt Shovel arm-in-arm, singing boisterously. Re-enter Manzo's, emerge with more beer. Start chanting and pointing a fans and making bellowing noises. Supporter with you children admonishes Briggs and Louis. Briggs and Lo jostle him. Louis pours beer on to his rosette. Briggs Louis attack man but are chased off by his children.

2.20pm: Briggs and Louis spoken to by uniformed officer for urinating against wall. Briggs squares up to officer, accusing him of being a jackbooted Nazi thug. Louis restrains him.

2.30pm: Undercover officers are now arm in arm, screaming obscenities and staring belligerently at fans outside the ground, saying: "Come on, we'll have the lot you" and "Fancy a bit do you?"

2.35pm: Two unidentified fans respond in the affirmative to this enquiry and give chase. Briggs and Louis are cornered in a back street and given what we in Football Intelligence call "a right good shoeing". Disturbance is spotted by lurking BNP troublemakers, triggering medium-scale violence among supporters.

2.40pm: Right wing activists exploit situation. Violence escalates. Police reserves with dogs drafted in. Water cannon mobilised, helicopter scrambled. All hospitals placed on emergency footing. Cars of the royal entourage are attacked by breakaway group led by Briggs and Louis. Army called out. RAF strike aircraft on stand-by.

2.55pm: Match postponed in the interests of public order.

4.20pm-midnight: Sporadic fighting still breaking out. Fire crews attempt to damp down buildings. Hostages released, most heavy artillery now impounded, core group of rioters taken into custody. Ring-leaders "The Governor" and "The General" (D. Briggs and R. Louis) placed in secure segregated cells. Queen makes television appeal for calm. Prime Minister visits scene of carnage. Copycat rioting erupts in most of UK's larger conurbations.

Arrests: 467   Injuries: Police 182, Civilians 63

INTERNAL AFFAIRS INTERVIEW TRANSCRIPT

TIME/DATE OF INTERVIEW; 4.45 on Friday July 16th 1995.

INTERVIEWEE; Anthony Robb-John.

RANK; Police Constable. **SUBJECT;** Briggs/Louis.

FILE; IA 126.

ANDREWS: You've been attached to 'C' Division for over a year, How do you find working with Briggs and Louis?

ARJ; I have never had the pleasure of working with them directly.

ANDREWS: But you must come across them in your day-to-day duties.

ARJ; Occasionally.

ANDREWS: And....

ARJ; And in spite of everything, I suppose I...admire their...sense of the absurd, their almost Jacques Tatti-esque ability to turn mundane situations into high comedy and low farce.

ANDREWS: Eh?

ARJ; They're a pair of clowns.

ANDREWS: You are prepared to say that on the record?

ARJ; I'm aware of the canteen culture that exists in this place, the idiotic bonds of loyalty that are supposed to make us all 'stick together', but frankly, I believe that incompetence and stupidity should not go unpunished. I don't see why the rest of us should always have to cover up for them.

ANDREWS: I see. So do you have any concrete examples of this 'incompetence and stupidity'?

ARJ; I hear stories.

ANDREWS: But have you personally any experience of....

ARJ; Look, as I'm sure you know only too well, 'old school' officers like Briggs and Louis have very little to do with we graduate intake newcomers. I think they see us as egg head upstarts. Therefore I have never been·invited to work on any of their operations.

ANDREWS: You get the impression that they are prejudiced against you because you are a university graduate.

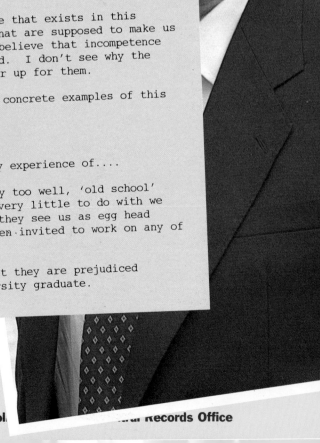

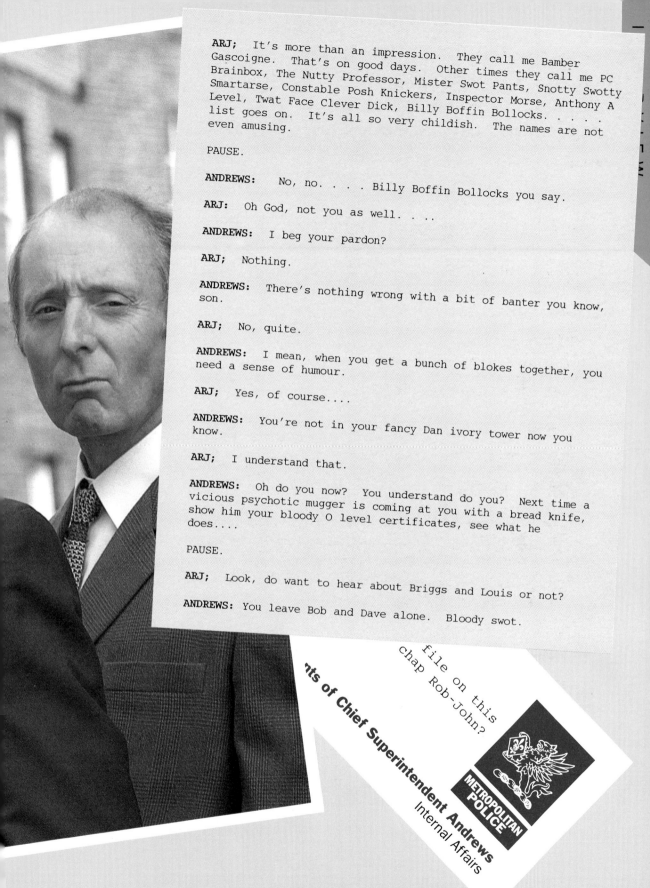

ARJ; It's more than an impression. They call me Bamber Gascoigne. That's on good days. Other times they call me PC Brainbox, The Nutty Professor, Mister Swot Pants, Snotty Swotty Smartarse, Constable Posh Knickers, Inspector Morse, Anthony A Level, Twat Face Clever Dick, Billy Boffin Bollocks. . . . . list goes on. It's all so very childish. The names are not even amusing.

PAUSE.

ANDREWS: No, no. . . . Billy Boffin Bollocks you say.

ARJ: Oh God, not you as well. . . .

ANDREWS: I beg your pardon?

ARJ; Nothing.

ANDREWS: There's nothing wrong with a bit of banter you know, son.

ARJ; No, quite.

ANDREWS: I mean, when you get a bunch of blokes together, you need a sense of humour.

ARJ; Yes, of course....

ANDREWS: You're not in your fancy Dan ivory tower now you know.

ARJ; I understand that.

ANDREWS: Oh do you now? You understand do you? Next time a vicious psychotic mugger is coming at you with a bread knife, show him your bloody O level certificates, see what he does....

PAUSE.

ARJ; Look, do want to hear about Briggs and Louis or not?

ANDREWS: You leave Bob and Dave alone. Bloody swot.

file on this
chap Rob-John?

...nts of Chief Superintendent Andrews
Internal Affairs

METROPOLITAN POLICE

Witness Statement
(CJ Act 1967, s.9 MC Act 1980, s.102, MC Rules 1981, r.70)

Statement of ....
Age if under 21 .... (if over 21 insert 'over 21'). Occupation ....

This statement (consisting of ..... pages each signed by me) is true to the best of my knowledge and belief and I make it knowing that, if it is tendered in evidence, I shall be liable to prosecution if I have wilfully stated in it anything that I know to be false or do not believe to be true.

Dated the   day of   19
Signature ....

'TOUGH GUYS DON'T LOOK BACK'
A nevil
by David Elmore Briggs

CHAPTER 21.

The sun was beating down on the centre court at Wimbledon. The crowd was eating strawberries and being excited. In the dressing room, Pete Sampras punched the metal cabinet thing where you leave your trousers and shoes.
"I can't do it Dave" he said.
"Of course you can Pete" Briggs said, punching him playfully on the arm.
"Just do all the things I told you to do. Make sure your back swing goes back properly, run around fast, hit the ball in the middle of your racket. Watch it doesn't hit the net."Pete Sampras smiled.
"You always have all the answers Dave" he said. "If it wasn't for that bullet in your leg that you picked up in 'Nam, it would be you out there playing in the Men's singles finals at Wimbledon."
Now it was Briggs' turn to smile. He stroked his bullet.
"In Vietnam they have a saying. Que sera sera."
A little bloke in a bowler hat came into the dressing room and said that the other bloke was already out on the court.
"Time to go Pete" Briggs said. "Win this one for me. And remember, tough guys don't look back" Pete started to walk out and Briggs said, 'oi, don't forget this' and he handed Pete Sampras his tennis racket. Sampras tutted.
"Where would I be without you" he said and he gave Briggs a manly hug. At that moment, Brigg's special bleeper went off. He ran out of

Signature ....Signature witnessed by ....

Property of the Metropolitan Police – Return to Central Records Office

...ntinuation of statement/Interview of ....

......the dressing room and had to run across centre court to get to

the exit, and the crowd all clapped like mad and said 'that's

him, that's Inspector Briggs, he could win Wimbledon if he

wanted but he's probably too busy catching crooks."

A minute later, Briggs was at the wheel of his massive Porsche,

in his sunglasses, chewing a match and smoking a cigar,

thinking, "I wonder what the Government wants me to do now!"

As it turned out, the Government wanted him to go and do

something secret. He had to go and sit in a park and wait for

somebody to come up and say some special words in code and

tell him what it was that he had to do and what it was was that

he had to go and solve a secret case. That's what he had to do.

And he went and did that.

So anyway, he caught a flight to ~~Kuala Lumpur~~ ~~Hong Kong~~

~~Moscow He had to go and walk around the zoo and find a~~

~~special monkey with He had to bring this piece of microfilm~~

~~back from~~ he had to go and expose Bob Louis as a spy. he had

to burst into his horrible flat that smelt of mice and feet and

beat him up until he admitted that he was indeed a spy and

that he had been working for foreigners all along. Briggs

knocked his pathetic fish tank over that was full of green water

with all the fish dead anyway and said, "the trouble with you,

Bob, is that you're too boring and ugly to ever get a girlfriend.

And for a start off you can forget about ever getting your

horrible dry flakey hands on Veronica from the mounted

division because I have been secretly sleeping with her for

years and we've never had the heart to tell you. And you

might think in your pathetic imagination that she prefers you

just because she danced with you at the last christmas party

but in fact she did that as a joke because she really fancies me

and can't stand you. How we laughed at you. It's me she likes.

So stop kidding yourself."

With that, Briggs swept out of Louis: flat and phoned Veronica.

"Hello darling" she said, "it's you I really love".

"Yes I'm aware of that" Briggs said, smiling, "let's get

married."

And they did. So piss off Louis.

..........................Signature witnessed by ....

Signature ....

M.P.93

**Chief Inspector Louis & Chief Inspector Briggs
The Nick
Crematorium Road
London WC2
0181-523 6743**

28 January 1995

To: The manager, Saatchi and Saatchi Advertising
London W1

Dear Sir/Madam,

We are two serving officers on the Metropolitan Police, but we also watch telly quite a lot. Admittedly, we are not experts, but we can't help noticing that a lot of the adverts these days are a bit rubbish. We have no intention of teaching our grandmother to make an omelette without breaking eggs, but having discussed the topic of the quality of adverts several times, we feel that we could have a go at doing a few ourselves. Some of the adverts we have come up with are, I think you'll agree, quite eye catching and probably could be used in your next 'campaign'. For example, Jaffa Cakes. Why not use the slogan, 'Hey mate, be a Jaffa Gaffer.' This slogan would suggest that by eating the said confectionery biscuit, you could become a 'gaffer' or boss. And of course, it rhymes. Also, Ford cars. You could show a Ford car crossing a shallow stream somewhere in the country and have the bloke say, 'Ford. . . perfect for crossing fords with.' Then there's beer adverts. We are yet to see one that tells you how quickly you can get drunk drinking the brand in question. How about 'You'll never remember a night spent drinking Special Brew.' And of course there's lamb. You are currently using the slogan 'Slam in the Lamb'. Fine. Nice rhyme. But how about this. "Oh damn, I forgot the lamb, now our Mam will have to give us bread and jam, and some spam. Wham bam bam.' The 'wham bam bam' bit might be a bit much, but you have to agree, there's something there. Should you decide to use any of the above, please call us on the number above and we will decide how much money we want. Thank you in anticipation,

Yours Sincerely

Robert Louise

Robert Louis

David Briggs

David Briggs.

from out... thanks for your inter... tell you all about the work of Saa... worldwide.

Yours sincerely

...chmer

...rate Affairs)

or Louis & Chief Inspector Briggs

...oad

...atchi and Saatchi Advertising

...Did we detect just a whiff of envy in your
... campaign ideas? We think we did. As a
...industry responsible for such pathetic
...'...apa', and 'there's juice loose aboot our
...that maybe you were so angry that we had
...'crack' at least four slogans that you decided to
...b us off with your daft brochure.We certainly wouldn't be
surprised if in the next few days, we don't see 'be a jaffa
gaffer' or our 'lamb' one on the telly, bold as brass. We've
heard about people nicking other people's ideas and getting
away with it. Well let us tell you Mr fancy bloody corporate
affairs manager (probably 'affairs has two meanings here,
knowing your sort), that if we do see any of our slogans on
the telly in the next few days, we might just accidentally
punch your name up onthe old police computer. Drive a car do
we Sir? Tax disc up to date is it Mr 'Loose Juice'? Have a
licence for our tv do we? We don't wish to get arsey with you
old son, but the next time some mugger is breaking into your
7 series BMW, don't be surprised if the boys in blue are a
bit slow getting up your private road to help out. We might
all be in the van, thinking up decent adverts.

Yours in disgust.

Robert Louis

Chief Inspector Louis

David Briggs

Chief Inspector Briggs.

SAATCHI & SAATCHI

Chief Inspectors Louis and Briggs
The Nick, Crematorium Road,
London WC2

3 February 1995

Dear Robert/David,

Thank you for your interest in our industry. Apologies
for the poor quality! As to your suggestions, I'm afraid
...the accounts you mention are in fact dealt with
...d there is no central 'clearing house'
...agencies employ
...ely with the

MEMORANDUM

FROM: Desk Sergeant Kent

TO: Superintendent Frank Cotta

RE: DC Briggs and DC Louis

Frank, the attached photo has b
to us, along with a ransom note
kidnapper has demanded ten thou
pounds in cash or Briggs and L
it'.

What should we do?
Sergeant Kent

with the compliments of Chief
Superintendent Andrews

METROPOLITAN
POLICE

aidi
. put
rd?

METROPOLITAN POLICE

MORANDUM

OM: Chief Superintendent Cottam

: Desk Sergeant Kent

ar Tom,

he important thing is that we don't rush into
nything. It's no good pandering to these people.
f we let him get away with this he'll probably do it
gain, but next time it might be real police
officers. I think we should just sit tight and see
what happens. In the meantime, you'd better make
Briggs and Louis' car parking spaces available to the
pool as they won't be using them. Also, reallocate
their work and see if you can get that dart board off
the wall of their office. I've always had my eye on
that. While you're in their office, you might as well
have a crack at their drinks cabinet. I know for a
fact that there is a bottle of single malt in there.
I'll have the malt, you have the Vodka and gin. The
beers can go to the Mounted Division.
Thanks for drawing this to my attention. Naturally,
our prayers are with Briggs and Louis at this
difficult time. If there is another ransom
note, bin it.

Best wishes,

Superintendent Cottam.

FROM THE DESK OF
SUPERINTENDENT FIELD

METROPOLITAN POLICE

PRELIMINARY ASSESSMENT.

RECRUIT; PC ROBERT LOUIS.

NOTES;

It is impossible for me to formulate a standard
assessment for this officer, since he was sent home
almost as soon as he reported for duty. The letter
which was sent to him stated clearly that he should
arrive at the station on Tuesday morning, prepared to
take up his role as an Assistant Beat Officer. As is
normal with these letters, this title was abbreviated
to ABO. PC Louis is the first and I hope the last
officer in my experience to fail to understand this
instruction. As the attached photo shows, Louis
reported for duty dressed as an Australian Aborigine or
'ABO'. I took the photo simply because I was sure that
if I didn't, no one would believe me.

Yours with astonishment,

Superintendent Field.

Property of the Metropolitan Police – Return to Central Records Office

Property of the Metropolitan Police – Return to Central Records Office

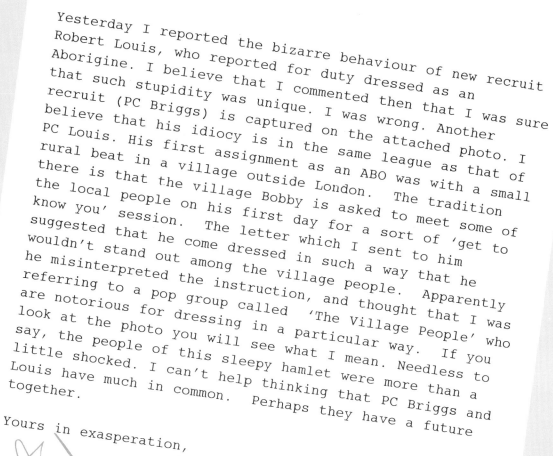

FROM THE DESK OF SUPERINTENDENT FIELD

METROPOLITAN POLICE

PRELIMINARY ASSESSMENT.

RECRUIT; DAVID BRIGGS.

NOTES;

Yesterday I reported the bizarre behaviour of new recruit Robert Louis, who reported for duty dressed as an Aborigine. I believe that I commented then that I was sure that such stupidity was unique. I was wrong. Another recruit (PC Briggs) is captured on the attached photo. I believe that his idiocy is in the same league as that of PC Louis. His first assignment as an ABO was with a small rural beat in a village outside London. The tradition there is that the village Bobby is asked to meet some of the local people on his first day for a sort of 'get to know you' session. The letter which I sent to him suggested that he come dressed in such a way that he wouldn't stand out among the village people. Apparently he misinterpreted the instruction, and thought that I was referring to a pop group called 'The Village People' who are notorious for dressing in a particular way. If you look at the photo you will see what I mean. Needless to say, the people of this sleepy hamlet were more than a little shocked. I can't help thinking that PC Briggs and Louis have much in common. Perhaps they have a future together.

Yours in exasperation,

Superintendent Field.

THE
Art and Craft
OF
Masonic
Practise

RECOGNISING A FELLOW MASON

Discretion is the key word here. The form of greeting illustrated to the right will be instantly detected by a practising member but go unnoticed by non-Masons. Such signs are not always strictly necessary. You will almost certainly be able to recognise a fellow Mason by his dignified demeanour, his noble bearing and his generous and polite personality. Other tell-tale signs to look out for: wearing a police uniform, saying "hello, hello" a lot, and regularly flexing at the knees.

MAKING CONTACT

As Masons, you will have many interests in common and much to discuss – charity work for instance, or awarding a forthcoming council road-building contract to a Masonic business associate. Masons are unafraid of human contact and regularly embrace. Not that we let any Nancy-boys in, of course. Or girls. Or Catholics come to that.

No area of Masonic ritual is more avidly discussed by the wider public than the Masonic Handshake. Some of the more outlandish "lay" theories provoke no end of amusement at Lodge meetings! In truth, there is no regulation handshake, though the clasp illustrated below has the advantage of being unlikely to arouse the suspicions of any non-Masons you may happen to meet in social situations.

MEETING THE CHIEF CONSTABLE

Masons are drawn from every conceivable walk of life, and at Lodge meetings social and class barriers are non-existent. You'll meet everyone from bankers to accountants, from solicitors to surveyors, and within this rich and diverse fraternity, titles are meaningless. Should you be lucky enough to encounter the

Chief Constable at the Lodge for instance, you can leave rank aside for the evening and simply address him as The Grand Wizard. You may even be asked to take part in the solemn and ancient ritual of "Beating In The Wizard".

Investment

The proudest day in a Mason's life is the day of his investment with the Sacred Apron of the Second and Third Fish. The new member swears fealty to Beth-Shi-Sumash, the ancient architect of the most sacred pyramids, and creator of the prelapsarian hallowed places. He also takes his vow of secrecy and promises to be regular with his monthly subs. The apron is, of course, a very visible reminder of the origins of the Craft – the trade of the venerated stonemasons. Its single, central pocket – or Kelth-Shmith – was the repository of the craftsmen's tools and yea unto this very day provides a useful cubby hole for loose change and darts.

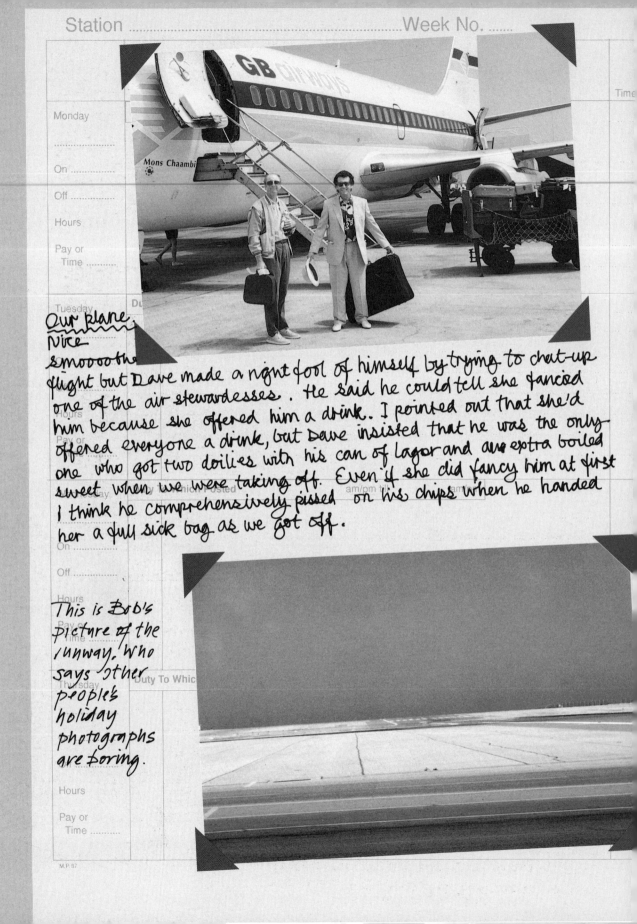

Our plane.
Nice
smooooth
flight but Dave made a right fool of himself by trying to chat-up
one of the air stewardesses. He said he could tell she fancied
him because she offered him a drink. I pointed out that she'd
offered everyone a drink, but Dave insisted that he was the only
one who got two doilies with his can of Lager and an extra boiled
sweet when we were taking off. Even if she did fancy him at first
I think he comprehensively pissed on his chips when he handed
her a full sick bag as we got off.

This is Bob's
picture of the
runway. Who
says other
people's
holiday
photographs
are boring.

The airport. The sign above our heads is Gibraltesarian for "Gibraltar Airport" (I pick up languages quite easily). We whizzed through customs in six hours flat on account of understandable suspicions about the size of Bob's "suitcase", or "handbag" as it is more accurately described. The men at customs wanted to know how he intended to make one pair of nylon underpants last a fortnight. I suggested that they search his bottom for contraband...

Me and Dave. To my right is the famous Rock of Gibraltar, and perched on top of it you can just see a nesting Ibis. Or it might be a satellite station. The Rock is very much a part of Britain and has been since we nicked it off the Dagos Spaniards thousands of years ago. In fact it's a little bit of Britain abroad, with proper British bobbies, a proud British branch of Marks & Sparks, plenty of good old British pubs, and pools of blooming British vomit on the pavement first thing in the morning. A proper home from home.

Bob is a picture of calm composure as he contemplates getting on Gibraltar's famous cable car. The journey up was frankly embarrassing. There we were, swaying about thousands of feet above the ground, supported, as I pointed out – only by a slender wire thread stretched to breaking point – and Bob was curled up on the floor of the cable car, weeping and being comforted by a toddler

What a waste of 1.50

The Super

Unfortunately, Sir decided it would be a good idea to join us for the second week. To be honest, it wasn't too bad. He spent the first day on the nudist beach where he fell into conversation with the Saga Holidays rep. Apparently they had much in common, on account of how her husband had just left her, just like Sir's wife is always leaving him. He didn't get much of a tan though, because they sat in bars all day drinking vodka, playing Jim Reeves records on the jukebox and occasionally bursting into tears.

...ucky I've got the sort of Italian
...d looks that mean I tan easily,
...reas Bob is more or less an
...no really. His appealing
...bination of white skin and
...age hair means he can only stay
...he sun for 0.5 of a second, and
...then if he's covered from head
...oe in sun factor 125, is wearing
...at, sunglasses and a one piece
...ing suit. And it's night time.
...s is Bob after he had "bobbed"!
...around in the Mediterranean for
...se on twelve hours following an
...fortunate jet-ski mishap. When
...got home three days later he
...s still giving off heat, like a
...rage radiator.

One of the famous
Gibraltar apes. That's
him on the right by the
way (ha!ha!). And on
the far right is what
seems to be one of
the slightly less
famous Gibraltar
giraffes. Dave enticed
the monkey over by
offering it a bag of
peanuts. This is the
same technique he
uses on new WPC's at the Christmas party. The only difference is
that none of the monkeys told him to piss off.

MEMORANDUM

FROM: DC David Briggs

TO: Commissioner Boyle

DATE: September 19 1991

Dear Your Highness,

RE: UNSOLVED MURDERS

I am most humbly sorry if I should in any way inconvenience you in the transmission of this epistle which I shall,mindful of the pressing nature of your available timepiece,   keep to the very minimum of brevity. I donm't know whether or not you have noticed the number of murders that are going un-solved nowadays.I know I have.anyway,watching the news at Ten last night I think I may have cracked it,and solved all outstanding murders. What struck me ,with my unsweving eye for such detail,was the news report about the latest tradgic murder slaying in a remote bit of dense woodland in the midlands.The local fuzz say that the body was found *by a man out walking his dog!(my italics).Now ask yourself,how many times is the body found by* a man out walking his dog?(still my italics).Yes,quite a lot isnt it?And a bit too much of a coincicidence to get past the wrinkly old nose of a seasoned investigator like Detective Constable(still!) David Briggs of c division.It would seem one man,together with his doggy accomplice,is going round the country carrying out all these murders and then simply pretending to have found his victim on an inocent walk.So,what I suggest we do is round up all men with dogs and beat them with rubber trucheons until one of them talks.The men that is,not the dogs.Though the dogs may eventully squeal.I hope this plan meets with your approval,and if you give me the merest hint of a nod from your noble head I will personally take over interrogation of subjects,while my aged assistant Bob Louis cleans up after their dogs.

Yours in most delightful anticipation of a favourable ripost,

DC briggs

Is this man an idiot or a lunatic or both? Get someone from psychological support services to give him — and his friend — the once over as a matter of urgency !!

TRANSCRIPT OF WORD ASSOCIATION TEST

SUBJECT(S): 936593 LOUIS
001634 BRIGGS

ATTENTION: COMMISSIONER DAVID BOYLE

I am currently conducting preliminary psychological and psychiatric
assessments of Detectives Briggs and Louis. I must assure you that
it is not normal practice to release details of investigations at
such an early stage, but in this particular case I thought an early
results appraisal might yield benefits all round. I attach a
transcript of their word association test.

Willis

Dr. Barbara Willis

BW: My name is Doctor Barbara Willis, and
Detectives David Briggs and Bob Louis. the ti
11.42 am.

DB: Is it on?

BW: What?

DB: The tape.

BW: Yes, I think so.

BL: Only we did that once.

BW: What?

BL: Thought we'd taped something but we hadn't. And it
confession, too.

DB (LAUGHS): Oh, yes, I remember now.

BL: When they played it in court it hadn't recorded p
instead of the confession it was that song "Clair" by Gil
Sullivan. We'd used an old tape from his car, you see .

DB: And it was our song.

BW: What, yours and his?

DB: No, no, no, nothing like that. At the time it
me and a very special young lady . . .

(continued)

BL: But hang on, that song's all about an old bloke going out
with a schoolgirl, isn't it?

DB: Not really.

BL: Well, how young exactly was this special lady?

DB: Look, when she was dressed up and covered in her fancy make-
up and it was dark nobody would ever for a minute imagine . . .

BW: OK, OK, guys, guys, guys, we're here to do a job right now.
What we're going to do is a simple word association test. When I say
a word, you just say the first word that comes into your mind, OK?

BL: Great.

BW: Right.

DB: Left.

BW: No, I haven't started yet. The next word I say
will be the start . . . woman.

BL: Mummy.

BW: Man.

DB: United.

BW: Hate.

BL: WPC Broadlady.

BW: Love.

DB: Boat.

BW: Food.

DB: Melons

W: Drink.

:   Yeah, great, why not? That didn't take long, Dave, did it?
at do you fancy, love? We'll get them in . . .

ording ends 11.44 am.

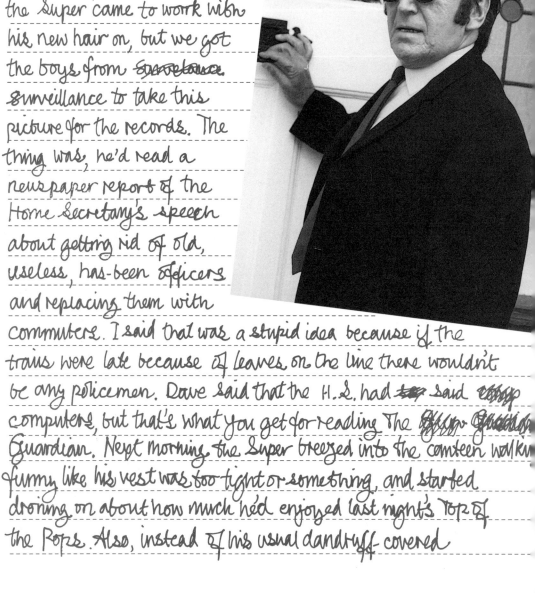

Nobody said anything the day
the Super came to work with
his new hair on, but we got
the boys from ~~surveillance~~
surveillance to take this
picture for the records. The
thing was, he'd read a
newspaper report of the
Home Secretary's ~~speech~~
about getting rid of old,
useless, has-been officers
and replacing them with
computers. I said that was a stupid idea because if the
trains were late because of leaves on the line there wouldn't
be any policemen. Dave said that the H.S. had ~~not~~ said ~~computers~~
computers, but that's what you get for reading The ~~Guardian~~ ~~Guardian~~
Guardian. Next morning the Super breezed into the canteen walking
funny like his vest was too tight or something, and started
droning on about how much he'd enjoyed last night's Top of
the Pops. Also, instead of his usual dandruff covered

Freeman's Catalogue sports jacket, he was wearing a flowery silk shirt, a cravat and a medallion. He looked like Huggy Bear off Starsky and Hutch. And he kept challenging all the younger officers to arm-wrestling contests. It was the day after that the rug made its first appearance. I must say I did feel a bit sorry for him. It was a very hot day, and the 2000 man-made fibres were obviously acting as some sort of thermal insulation on the top of his head, causing the glue to melt and run down his face in little black rivulets, and his forehead to go puce. It obviously itched like buggery as well. That said, everyone was just getting used to the new-look Super, when heat build-up within the rug obviously reached critical mass, and it started to spontaneously combust, sending a little cloud of blue smoke into the air. Of course, nobody wanted to be the one to point this out, so it was left to muggins here to pour the cup of tea over his head and put it out. Not wanting to draw attention to the wig I quickly made up a cover story, pretending that I thought I'd spotted a rabid meercat creeping up behind him with its fangs bared and was attempting to frighten it off with cold tea. Was he grateful? Was he heck! I agree with the Home Secretary, it's time to cut out the dead wood and replace them with computers who don't wear wigs and who don't put you on traffic duty if you pour tea all over them.

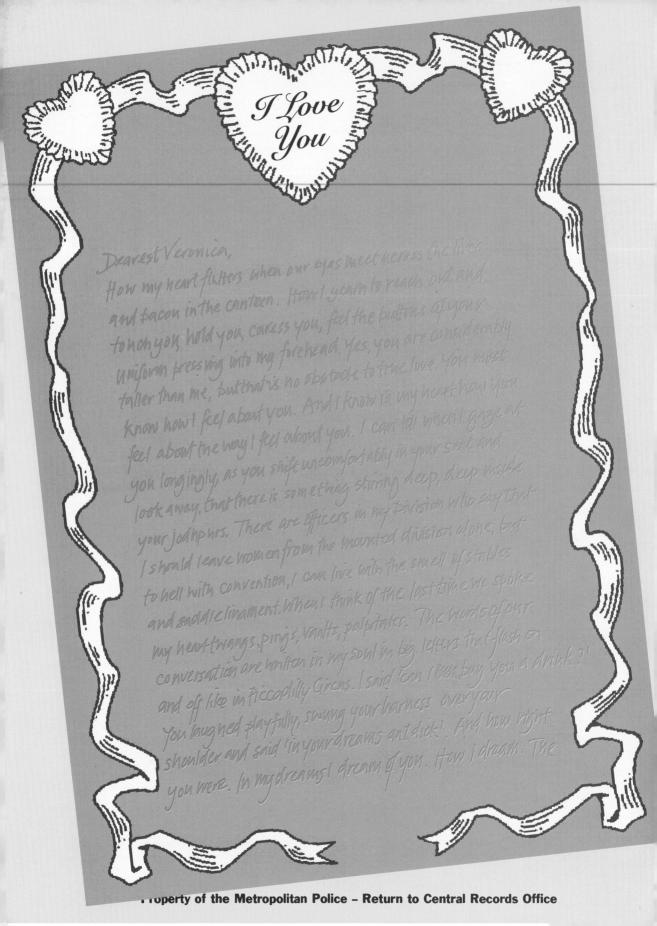

Dearest Veronica,

How my heart flutters when our eyes meet across the liver and bacon in the canteen. How I yearn to reach out and touch you, hold you, caress you, feel the buttons of your uniform pressing into my forehead. Yes, you are considerably taller than me, but that's no obstacle to true love. You must know how I feel about you. And I know in my heart how you feel about the way I feel about you. I can tell when I gaze at you longingly, as you shift uncomfortably in your seat and look away, that there is something stirring deep, deep inside your jodhpurs. There are officers in my Division who say that I should leave women from the mounted division alone, but to hell with convention, I can live with the smell of stables and saddle liniment. When I think of the last time we spoke my heart twangs, pings, vaults, palpitates. The words of our conversation are written in my soul in big letters that flash on and off like in Piccadilly Circus. I said 'can I buy you a drink?' You laughed playfully, swung your harness over your shoulder and said 'in your dreams ant dick'. And how right you were. In my dreams I dream of you. How I dream. The

I Love You

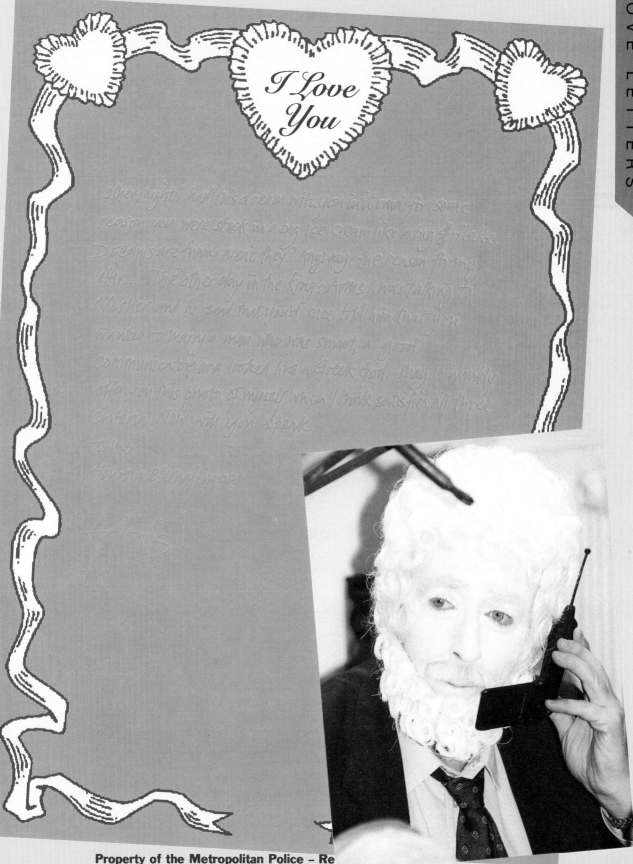

One night I had this dream with you in it and for some reason you were stuck in a big ice cream like a big Flake. Dreams are funny aren't they? Anyway, the reason for my letter ... The other day in the King's Arms I was talking to Mosher and he said that your sister told him that you wanted to marry a man who was smart, a good communicator and looked like a Greek God. May I humbly offer you this photo of myself which I think satisfies all three criteria. Now will you speak to me.

Yours undying hope

Denis

Dear Veronica,

I have just discovered that my junior assistant, R.C. Briggs, has been writing stupid letters to you. I'm sorry. He doesn't realise that it is me you love, not him, but he's like that. If I have anything, he wants to have it as well. He's the same with Crunchies. I go to the shop and I say 'do you want anything from the shop?' and he goes 'oh no sir' in that stupid whining voice of his. Then, when I get back from the shop with my Daily Mirror and my Crunchie, he goes 'ooooh, Bob, can I have a bit of your crunchie?' Well, he's not having a bit of my crunchie. Not now, not ever. You are my Crunchie Veronica and I want to have you all to myself. There's no point pretending you don't love me. I can see it in your eye... (by the way.. I find the patch on your other eye very attractive). The other day in the King's Arms, I was speaking to Nosher who says he knows you. He told me that you'd once commented that you liked bold, aggressive men who wouldn't let other people push them around. You also said you liked men in uniform and you especially liked men who drove really powerfull vehicles.. since my pathetic male secretary Briggs sent you a photo, I've had one done myself. I think this will do the trick. Does this mean that we are officially going out ??

Yours forever

Bob

METROPOLITAN POLICE

MEMORANDUM

FROM: DI REEVES (VICE SQUAD)

TO: Superintendent Cottam

Is there no end to the capacity of your men to spoil and interfere with other units' operations? For ten months, we have been carrying out an undercover surveillance operation in one of Soho's most notorious leather and bondage clubs. In that time we had been carefully preparing a midnight raid on the club, hoping to net the pimps, drug dealers and pornographers who frequent the place.   The date of the raid was kept relatively secret, but surely someone in your Division must have known.   Was it coincidence then that on the night of the raid, the club was being used by two of your officers for a party celebrating 25 years in the service? When we made our arrests, we soon discovered that our haul consisted of seven PCs, six WPCs, a dozen DCs, three Detective Inspectors and, of course, one

continued

Superintendent (I hardly need remind you, Frank, of who that was). The two DCs responsible for throwing the party were captured on stage by one of our undercover surveillance cameras. I trust that suitable disciplinary action will be taken. I should also tell you (in strictest confidence) that in one of the backrooms of the club we also picked up Commissioner Boyle. Far be it from me to jump to conclusions, but I was asured by other partygoers that the Commissioner wasn't on any guest list, and that he had no knowledge that the party was taking place. He appeared to be there for reasons of his own. He was dressed as an Armadillo, clad from head to foot in leather, chained to a large hairdress Luton.

Yours in bewilderment

THE METROPOLITAN POLICE
Human Resource Department

METROPOLITAN POLICE

25 YEAR REVIEW

SUBJECT: DC ROBERT LOUIS

YEARS OF SERVICE: 24 YEARS, 8 MONTHS

NOTES;

As is customary, all officers
approaching 25 years of service are
given a thorough review to establish
their suitability for a renewal of
their contract of employment. When DC
Louis was told that his age might
become a factor, he began to behave
oddly. He began to report for duty on
a small bicycle, he attempted to
cultivate an interest in popular music
and he tried to insinuate that he was
suffering from acne by dotting his face
with red and yellow marker pen.On the
day of his review, his appearance, was,
to say the least, unusual. The
attached photo illustrates my point.

THE METROPOLITAN POLICE
Human Resource Department

IN REFERRING LOUIS' CASE BACK TO HIS
SUPERINTENDENT, I WAS TOLD THAT EVEN
AS A YOUNG MAN, LOUIS HAD NEVER BEEN
SUITABLE FOR HIS POSITION AS A POLICE
OFFICER, AND THAT AGE WAS THE LEAST
OF HIS PROBLEMS. I THEREFORE
RECOMMEND THAT WE CONTINUE WITH HIS
CONTRACT OF EMPLOYMENT, IF ONLY TO
PROVIDE A LITTLE WELCOME LIGHT RELIEF
INTO A HARD PRESSED, HIGH STRESS
MODERN POLICE FORCE.

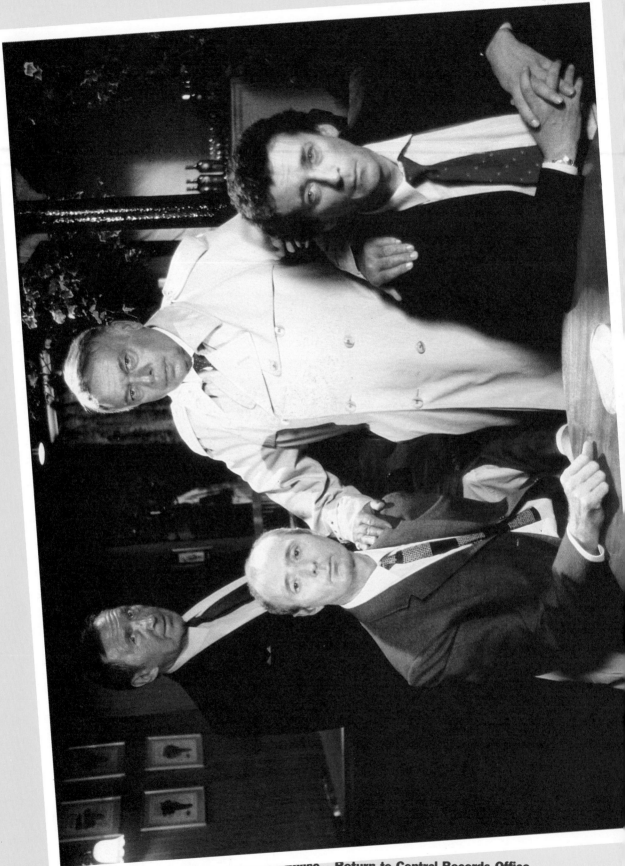